Iran

Iran

BY MIRIAM GREENBLATT

Enchantment of the World
Second Series

Children's Press®

A Division of Scholastic Inc.

NEW YORK   TORONTO   LONDON   AUCKLAND   SYDNEY
MEXICO CITY   NEW DELHI   HONG KONG
DANBURY, CONNECTICUT

Frontispiece: A carpet seller mends a rug in his shop

Consultant: Amy J. Johnson, Ph.D., Assistant Professor of History, Berry College, Mount Berry, Georgia

Please note: All statistics are as up-to-date as possible at the time of publication.

Book production by Herman Adler Design

Library of Congress Cataloging-in-Publication Data

Greenblatt, Miriam.
    Iran / by Miriam Greenblatt
      p. cm. — (Enchantment of the world. Second series)
    Includes bibliographical references and index.
    ISBN 0-516-22375-5
    1. Iran—Juvenile literature. [1. Iran.] I. Title. II. Series.
DS254.75 .I73 2003
955—dc21   2001008320

Acknowledgments

In writing this book, I was fortunate enough to be helped by a number of Iranians both in the United States and in Iran. I thank Job Youshaei, who lent me books about Iran from his personal library and who sold me my first Persian carpet. Mina Danesh reviewed the material on Iranian weddings. Tour guide Saeid Haji-Hadi provided a wealth of information about his country's history and culture during my visit to Iran. Many Iranians talked to me about their feelings, experiences, and hopes for the future.

Cover photo:
Jame Mosque,
Yazd

Contents

An extended family

Parthian sculpture

A Different Kind of Revolution

ARLY IN 1979, A REVolution took place in the Middle Eastern nation of Iran. It was symbolized by two airplane flights: the first from Iran to Egypt, the second from France to Iran.

On January 16, the king of Iran, Mohammad Reza Shah Pahlavi, arrived at the airport in the capital city of Tehran. A silver and blue Boeing 707, loaded with hundreds of pieces of luggage, sat on the runway. Among the luggage was a box filled with Iranian soil. The shah got out of his car and was immediately surrounded by officers and friends. One by one, they kissed his hand, as tears streamed down his face. The shah and his wife then boarded the plane and took off for Egypt. The trip was supposedly a "vacation" of unknown length. It was to last for the rest of the shah's life.

Shah Pahlavi leaves Iran for Egypt shortly before Khomeini's return.

Opposite: **Rioters burn a portrait of Shah Pahlavi as a sign of protest against his regime.**

A Different Kind of Revolution   **9**

About two weeks later, on February 1, a Boeing 747 left Paris, France, for Tehran. Aboard was the Ayatollah Ruhollah Khomeini, the leader of the revolution. (*Ayatollah*, or religious leader, is the highest rank an Iranian Muslim cleric can achieve.) The shah had exiled Khomeini from Iran in 1964.

Ayatollah Khomeini arrives in Tehran.

However, while in exile, the ayatollah sent his supporters messages on cassette tapes urging them to challenge the shah's government. Also aboard the airplane were 47 of Khomeini's closest followers, plus 141 journalists. According to the laws of the religion of Islam, no alcohol was served during the flight. Women journalists covered their hair with scarves.

Some 1 million Iranians turned out to greet Khomeini and welcome him home. The crowds were so thick that the

Geopolitical map of Iran

IRAN

- Cities of over 200,000 people
- Smaller cities and towns

0   200 miles
0   300 kilometers

KAZAKHSTAN

UZBEKISTAN

ARMENIA

AZERBAIJAN

CASPIAN SEA

TURKMENISTAN

Tabriz

L. Urmia

Safid R.

Rasht

Gorgan

Tehran

Mashhad

Hamadan

Qom

Dasht-e-Kavir

Zayandeh R.

Na'in

Esfahan

Dasht-e-Lut

Karun R.

Yazd

AFGHANISTAN

Abadan

Kerman

IRAQ

Takht-e Jamshid (Persepolis)

Shatt-al-Arab R.

Shiraz

Bam

PAKISTAN

KUWAIT

PERSIAN GULF

Bandar-e Abbas

Strait of Hormuz

GULF OF OMAN

Iran

U.A.E.

SAUDI ARABIA

OMAN

ayatollah's transportation could not drive through the streets of Tehran. He had to be transferred to a helicopter instead.

Khomeini's first act was to visit the Behesht-e Zahra cemetery, Tehran's main burial ground. There he paid tribute to the "martyrs" who had been killed by the shah's secret police. The ayatollah's second act was to declare the shah's government illegal and set up his own rival government. Khomeini then called on the army to support him.

The fighting lasted for several days, during which time 500 lives were lost. However, Khomeini and his followers were victorious. Tehran Radio announced: "This is the voice of Tehran, the voice of true Iran, the voice of revolution. The dictatorship has come to an end."

Like most revolutions, the Iranian Revolution had many political, social, and economic causes. What made this revolution different was its religious nature. Iran not only abolished its 2,500-year-old monarchy; it also established a government that combines religion and the state. This kind of government is called a *theocracy*. Iran is the first theocracy in modern times.

A Difficult Environment

I RAN IS A DIFFICULT PLACE IN WHICH TO LIVE. DESERTS AND mountains dominate the landscape. Rainfall is light, rivers are few, and all the lakes are salty.

Iran is one of the largest countries in the Middle East. Its total land area is almost 636,000 square miles (about 1,648,000 square kilometers), making it one-sixth the size of the United States.

Iran is bordered on the north by the Caspian Sea, as well as by three countries that were formerly part of the Soviet Union: Armenia, Azerbaijan, and Turkmenistan. To the east, Iran shares borders with Afghanistan and Pakistan. The Persian Gulf and the Gulf of Oman (which widens into the Arabian Sea) wash Iran's southern border. To the west lie Turkey and Iraq.

Iran's southern border meets the Persian Gulf.

The Iranian Plateau

The central part of Iran is a plateau, or high plain. This stretch of flat land occupies almost half the country. It is one of the driest and most desolate areas in the world. Two deserts found here are the Dasht-e-Kavir and the Dasht-e-Lut.

The Dasht-e-Kavir is a desert of salt about 500 miles (800 km) long and about 200 miles (320 km) wide. A thick white crust of salt crystals lies on top of quicksand. This glittery crust is formed when rains or floodwaters from the mountains dissolve the salt in the quicksand and then dry up. During the time when caravans followed the Silk Road across from China to Europe, the Dasht-e-Kavir was one of the most dangerous parts of the journey. Not only was the salt surface of the desert

The Dasht-e-Kavir is about the size of California.

painful to walk on; it often cracked wide open. Then camels and traders alike fell into the quicksand beneath and perished.

A valley lies at the base of the Zagros Mountains.

The Dasht-e-Lut is a desert of sand, about 300 miles (480 km) long and about 200 miles (320 km) wide. It contains neither trees, bushes, nor flowers. Bunches of tough camel grass grow here and there. Occasionally you can spot a lizard skittering for shelter behind a rock. Most of the area is an empty wasteland.

Iran's Mountains

Surrounding Iran's central plateau are three large mountain ranges. Like the plateau, they cover almost half the country. Most Iranians live within sight of some mountain.

The Zagros Mountains are 1,100 miles (1,770 km) long. They run along Iran's western and southern borders. From the

Mount Demavand, which is snow-capped year round, is Iran's most popular mountain for climbing.

air, they look something like a washboard, with row after row of jagged peaks, each higher than the one before. Between the rows lie long, narrow valleys with flat floors. A few roads cross the Zagros from east to west, but in general, travel here is difficult.

The Elburz Mountains are 560 miles (900 km) long. They curve from Iran's northeast corner along the Caspian Sea to the country's northwest corner. Many peaks are covered with snow all year round. The tallest peak is Mount Demavand, a volcano that towers 18,934 feet (5,771 meters) above sea level. If you climb to the top of Mount Demavand, you can smell the sulphurous gas that oozes out of its cone. The Iranians who lived here 3,000 years ago had a legend about this gas. They said it was the bad breath of an evil tyrant who had been captured by a great hero and imprisoned within the cone.

Iran's third major mountain range is the Kopet range. It runs for more than 400 miles (645 km) along the country's border with Turkmenistan.

Earthquake!

"I was outside when I heard the mountain roar like a dragon and suddenly the air became dark as night from the thick cloud of dust."

The speaker was Ghodamreza Nowrouz-Zadeh. He was describing the powerful earthquake that hit Iran in May 1997. The quake, which measured 7.3 on the Richter scale, killed at least 2,400 people and injured an estimated 6,000. About 200 villages were either destroyed or severely damaged. Water and power lines were cut. All six of Nowrouz-Zadeh's grand-children died when their schoolhouse collapsed.

The quake triggered landslides, making it impossible for the rescue workers to use the region's narrow dirt roads.

Unfortunately, Iran lies in an earthquake zone. Each year hundreds of small tremors shake the land. About every ten to twelve years, the country is struck by a major quake.

The Lowlands

The small part of Iran that is neither plateau nor mountains consists of two coastal lowlands. One lies north of the Elburz Mountains along the Caspian shoreline. The other lies along the coast of the Persian Gulf.

Rivers and Qanats

Iran has three main rivers. The longest is the Karun, at about 528 miles (850 km) long. It winds down the western slope of the Zagros Mountains and then flows south to the Iran-Iraq border. There it joins another river, the Shatt-al-Arab, then empties into the Persian Gulf. The Karun is Iran's only navigable river, but it is so shallow that boats can travel only a few miles from its mouth.

A second river, the Zayandeh, is about 250 miles (400 km) long. It flows down the eastern slope of the Zagros Mountains and into a salt marsh in the interior. The word *zayandeh* means "life giving." The river got its name because it brings water to the oasis of Esfahan, one of Iran's major cities and a former capital.

The third main river, the Safid, is about 450 miles (720 km) long. It flows north from the Elburz Mountains into the Caspian Sea. Dams built along the Safid's steep descent furnish hydroelectric power and water for irrigation.

Iran also has many small rivers and streams. Most of them, however, dry up in summer. As a result, people have to get their water from springs and melting snow from the mountains. The water is brought to their houses and

Iran's Geographical Features

Highest Elevation: Mount Demavand, 18,934 feet (5,771 m)

Lowest Elevation: 92 feet (28 m) below sea level, along the coast of the Caspian Sea

Greatest Distance North to South: 810 miles (1,296 km)

Greatest Distance East to West: 860 miles (1,376 km)

Longest River: Karun, about 528 miles (850 km)

Largest Lake: Urmia, 1,737 square miles (4,701 sq km)

Longest Mountain Chain: Zagros, about 1,100 miles (1,770 km)

Largest City (est. 2002): Tehran, 10,000,000

Highest Average Temperature: 122°F (50°C), in the plateau region of southern Iran

Lowest Average Temperature: -20°F (-29°C), in the mountainous region of northwestern Iran

RUSSIA
KAZAKHSTAN
UZBEKISTAN
TURKEY
ARMENIA
AZERBAIJAN
CASPIAN SEA
TURKMENISTAN
Tabriz
L. Urmia
Safid R.
Rasht
KOPET RANGE
Mt. Demavand
Tehran
ELBURZ MTNS.
Mashhad
Hamadan
Qom
Dasht-e-Kavir
KHORASAN RANGE
AFGHANISTAN
Esfahan
IRANIAN PLATEAU
Dasht-e-Lut
Karun R.
ZAGROS MTNS.
Zayandeh R.
IRAQ
Abadan
Shiraz
Shatt-al-Arab R.
PAKISTAN
KUWAIT
PERSIAN GULF
QATAR
GULF OF OMAN
SAUDI ARABIA
U.A.E.
OMAN

0   200 miles
0   300 kilometers

Women wash dishes and children splash happily in an artificial pond.

fields by *qanats*, or canals. These are dug underground. If they were on the surface, the water would evaporate in the hot sun.

Qanats are anywhere from half a mile (0.8 km) to 50 miles (80 km) long. At regular intervals, narrow shafts lead from the tunnel up to the surface. The shafts enable workers to enter the tunnel to remove loose dirt and keep the tunnel's walls from caving in. The workers pile the dirt around the shaft openings. If you view the openings from the air, they look like a string of doughnuts stretching between the village and the mountains.

Digging qanats is usually a family occupation that is handed down from father to son. Iranians have been getting water this way for about 2,500 years.

Some Salty Lakes

Like all of Iran's lakes, the Caspian Sea is salty. It is the world's largest inland sea at 144,000 square miles (373,000 sq km). Almost five times the size of the second-largest lake, Lake Superior in America, it contains about 45 percent of all the lake water in the world.

Horseback riders enjoy an outing on a Caspian Sea beach.

In the past, the Caspian Sea was a major source of caviar, or salted fish eggs. Since caviar is both delicious and expensive, its export earned Iran a great deal of money. In recent years, however, pollution from oil leaks and other industrial waste have greatly reduced the number of sturgeon from which the eggs come.

Iran and the other nations that border the Caspian Sea—Azerbaijan, Kazakhstan, Russia, and Turkmenistan—have formed a regional association to improve trade and transportation across the Caspian. Perhaps these nations will also work together to reduce the sea's pollution.

Lake Urmia is the largest lake, 1,737 square miles (4,701 sq km), completely within Iran. Its water consists of almost 25 percent minerals, or about seven times as much as the ocean, and is much too bitter to drink. However, soaking in the mineral-rich water helps to relieve rheumatism. Several spas have been built along the lakeshore for those needing therapy.

Fish cannot survive in Lake Urmia. However, thousands of birds, especially flamingos, use it as a stopping place during their north-south migration each year. The United Nations has helped to protect the migratory birds by declaring Lake Urmia an "area of special interest."

A Variety of Climates

Most of Iran is dry. Rain falls only from November through March. The plateau receives less than 12 inches (30.5 centimeters) of rain a year, while the deserts receive less than 5 inches (12.7 cm). The only region with abundant rainfall is the lowland along the Caspian Sea. With year-round rainfall, it receives 40–60 inches (100–150 cm) of rain annually.

Winds assail Iran from all directions. Warm, damp winds blow from Saudi Arabia year round. In winter, cold, dry winds blow southward from Siberia. In summer, the so-called 120-day wind brings scorching heat from Pakistan.

The different regions of Iran have different climates. In general, the plateau is burning hot in summer and bitterly cold in winter. Temperature readings of 120° Fahrenheit (48.6° Celsius) are common in July and August. In December and January, the thermometer sometimes plunges to 35°F below 0°F (–37°C).

In contrast, temperatures in the northern coastal lowland range from the mid-40s°F (about 5°C) in winter to the mid-70s°F (about 25°C) in summer. Because of the mild climate, as well as the abundant rainfall, approximately one out of five Iranians call this region home.

The southern coastal lowland is extremely hot and humid most of the year. Temperatures average 122°F (50°C). One traveler described the region as having "frying-pan" weather! December through February, however, are very pleasant with a temperature of about 64°F (18°C), and wealthy Iranians from the north often go south for the winter.

The mountainous regions of Iran, like the plateau, have very cold, harsh winters with many below freezing temperatures. Some places become cut off by snow for weeks at a time. Summers in the mountains, however, are comparatively mild. Temperatures seldom go above 80°F (27°C).

Forests, Flowers, and Wildlife

The tale of Iran's plants and animals is a tale of forests that have been cut down and species that no longer exist. It is also a tale about people whose idea of paradise is a garden where flowers bloom in splendor and where one tree is said to be so large that a man can ride in its shade for a hundred years.

Vegetation is sparse because most of Iran is dry. However, about 10 percent of the country is heavily forested. Oaks and fragrant junipers cover many of the peaks in the Zagros Mountains. Hardwood trees such as beech, elm, oak, and pine can be found on the northern slope of the Elburz Mountains. Tropical mangroves flourish along the Caspian Sea, while palm trees grow in the southern coastal lowland. Farmers cultivate almond, pistachio, and walnut trees wherever they can, for the nuts are a good cash crop.

Opposite: **A mother and children enjoy the garden at the tomb of the poet Saadi.**

A solitary pistachio tree in central Iran.

Forests in Iran were much more widespread in the past. Grazing herds of sheep and goats caused considerable damage to the land. So, too, did many of the country's nomads and villagers, who cut down trees and either burned them to make charcoal for fuel or used them for building houses. Accordingly, in 1962 the Iranian government took over ownership of all the country's forests. Since then, it has tried to improve the way Iranians use their forest resources.

Useful and Beautiful Plants

In Iran's arid and semiarid areas, the vegetation consists primarily of shrubs. Most have thorns, which help prevent moisture from evaporating. Some shrubs—such as absinthe, poppy, and sesame—are used to add flavor in cooking. Other shrubs—such as indigo and saffron—produce dyes for coloring textiles.

Iranians are passionate about flowers and try to grow them wherever they can because so much of their land is barren. The most popular flower is the rose, especially the double pink

Many Iranians regard the rose as their national flower.

and the double yellow varieties. Both of these varieties probably originated in Iran. Iranians have always shown roses in their carpets and miniature paintings. Poets have often written about roses. Other flowers common to the country include the bellflower, buttercup, crocus, gentian, geranium, grape hyacinth, poppy, and tulip.

An Abundant Wildlife

When Iran was a mighty empire, one of its symbols was the Asiatic lion. Today, the lion no longer lives in Iran. Also probably extinct in Iran is the tiger, although there have been rumors of tiger sightings along the Caspian Sea. However, leopards can still be found in southeastern Iran, and panthers still roam the forests. The forests are also home to antelope, hyenas, porcupines, and wild boars.

Hyena and her cub

Alborz red sheep are known for their large spiral horns.

Two unusual animals are the Alborz red sheep and the Oreal ram. Both boast large spiral horns. Among the animals on the international endangered species list are the Asian cheetah, the Asian black bear, and the Persian fallow deer.

At one time, Iran was a bird-watcher's paradise. Millions of native birds filled the sky. Twice a year, additional millions of birds migrated to and from Europe and Russia, spending the winter along the Caspian Sea. In recent years, however, farmers have drained many marshes and converted them into farmland. This, combined with the loss of forests, has destroyed much of the birds' natural habitat. As a result, the bird population has fallen drastically.

The Asian Black Bear

The Asian black bear has such long hair on its neck and shoulders that it looks as if it were wearing a collar. Although most of its fur is pitch black, it has a large white mark on its chest. It lives in the forest. In fact, it prefers to spend much of its time up a tree rather than on the ground. It eats mostly ants, berries, fruit, and seeds. Each family group—consisting of a mother and her cubs—has its own territory. If another bear intrudes, the mother bear quickly chases it away.

National Parks

Iran has about seventy national parks, wildlife refuges, and places that have been set aside to protect wetlands. However, in most cases, these areas are not patrolled by rangers. There are not even laws to prevent hunting or development. Asian black bears live in Mehrouyeh National Park, in central Iran. Two parks, Bakhtegan and Assad Abad, specialize in providing homes for birds.

Nevertheless, some species of birds are still common. Golden eagles soar above the ground. Pink flamingos breed along the Persian Gulf. Exotic natives include the red-wattled lapwing, the yellow partridge, the black kite, and the white-throated robin.

Pink flamingos wade in the waters of the Persian Gulf.

An agama lizard at home in the desert of central Iran.

Iran is rich in fish and shellfish. In addition to sturgeon, the Caspian Sea contains twenty-nine other fish species, including salmon, carp, and pike. The Persian and Oman Gulfs boast some 200 species of fish, as well as lobster and shrimp.

Iran is also rich in reptiles, including frogs, lizards, turtles, and snakes. Some of the snakes are poisonous, and people take great care to avoid them. The Greek tortoise waddles around almost everywhere.

From Empire to Islamic Republic

As ONE OF THE OLDEST COUNTRIES IN THE WORLD, Iran has had a long and eventful history. Over the centuries, its borders have changed frequently. At times Iran was a mighty empire, ruling lands as far apart as Egypt and India. At other times, Iran itself was ruled by foreign invaders. For most of its past, Iran was a monarchy. In 1979 it became a republic run by Muslim clerics.

Opposite: **Castle and ruins of the old city of Bam.**

Most historians begin Iran's history about 6000 B.C.E. At that time, the land at the head of the Persian Gulf and part of the Iranian plateau were filled with many small agricultural villages. In addition to farming, the inhabitants of these villages had domesticated sheep, goats, and other livestock. They had also developed pottery and metalworking.

Stone relief of Elamite archers marching into battle.

By about 3000 B.C.E., the Elamites were flourishing in southwest Iran. Many Elamites lived in cities. Some of them could read and write. They had an organized priesthood and were ruled by a hereditary king. They were also good fighters, who gradually extended their power eastward across the plateau.

In the meantime, starting about 1500 B.C.E., groups of people began migrating into Iran from the north. They were sometimes called Indo-Europeans and sometimes called Aryans (from which we get the name *Iran*, meaning "land of the Aryans"). Among them were some nomadic herders who eventually settled in southern Iran. Since the region in which they settled was called Pars or Parsa, they became known as Persians.

By 500 B.C.E., the Persians were no longer just herders of cattle and sheep. Under the Achaemenid dynasty, or family of rulers, they had established the first world empire. Covering an area from India to Egypt, this empire measured almost 3,000 miles (7,769 km) from east to west and 500–1,500 miles (1,294–3,884 km) from north to south. Among its conquests was the fabled city of Babylon, which had previously controlled much of the Middle East.

Through Cyrus the Great's ingenuity, Babylon fell under the rule of the Persian Empire.

Cyrus the Great

The king who conquered Babylon was Cyrus the Great, who ruled for twenty-nine years, from 558 B.C.E. to 529 B.C.E. Most people had believed that Babylon could not be taken. It was not only strongly walled and fortified but also protected by a deep, swiftly flowing river. Cyrus was clever, though. He ordered his soldiers to dig dozens of small channels that drained the river until it ran no higher than a man's thigh. The Persian army was then able to wade through the river and capture the city.

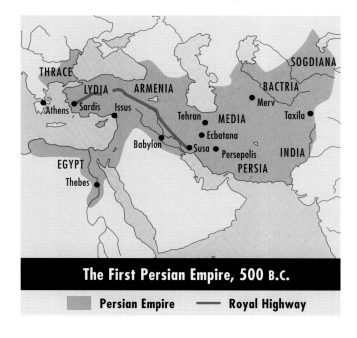

The First Persian Empire, 500 B.C.

Persian Empire — Royal Highway

To celebrate his victory, Cyrus held a magnificent triumphal procession through Babylon. It included bulls and white horses to be sacrificed; priests carrying a sacred fire; 4,000 lancers; horses with bridles of gold; and of course the king in his chariot, wearing a blue tunic, scarlet trousers, and a purple cloak.

Cyrus was a remarkably fair and generous ruler. He allowed the peoples he conquered to keep their own language, religious beliefs, holidays, and laws. He felt that this policy would make them far less likely to revolt. He also allowed thousands of Jews, who had been exiled from Jerusalem when it was captured by the Babylonians, to return to their ruined capital.

Cyrus the Great

A New Military Technique

In the past, generals in the Middle East used horses only to pull chariots, each of which carried one or two soldiers. Persian generals, in contrast, put their soldiers on horseback. This made the Persian armies much more mobile than the armies of their opponents. Persian troops could move quickly from one part of the battlefield to another and could take advantage of any break in the enemy lines.

Achaemenid king Darius I

Darius

The next great Achaemenid king was Darius I, who ruled for thirty-five years, from 521 B.C.E. to 486 B.C.E. After putting down a series of revolts, he turned his attention to reorganizing the Persian Empire.

Darius divided the empire into provinces. Each province was headed by three men: a governor, a secretary, and a general. These officials collected taxes and settled local disputes. Since each official reported to Darius separately, the king was able to check on whether or not the officials were honest. In addition, a group of inspectors known as "The Eyes and Ears of the King" would pay surprise visits to the officials to make certain that they were doing a good job.

Darius built the first great highway system in the world. Called the Royal Highway, the roads were paved with stone and were wide enough for

Golden Coins

In addition to good roads, an important aid to trade was a gold coin called a *daric*, in honor of Darius. History's first coins had been minted in the kingdom of Lydia, in what is now Turkey. After conquering Lydia, Darius decided to adopt its system of coined money. Each daric contained a fixed amount of gold. That way, anyone using it knew exactly how much it was worth.

four horses to ride abreast. Post stations stood along the roads, a day's ride apart. Messengers galloping from one station to the next carried the king's orders quickly to all parts of the empire. In addition to post stations, Darius set up forts and had the roads patrolled by soldiers on horseback. Safe roads meant that caravans bearing goods and taxes could travel without fear of bandits.

In addition to a system of roads, Darius began construction of one of the most magnificent cities of the ancient world. We know it by its Greek name, Persepolis. Iranians call it *Takht-e Jamshid*, or "Throne of Jamshid," after a mythical king.

Ruins of Persepolis

Persepolis was built on top of some limestone hills beside a small river. It contained temples, palaces, storehouses, and barracks for the imperial guards. It had running water and a sewage system. There were no houses for ordinary people, though. That was because the city was primarily a religious center.

Each year, at the time of the Persian New Year in spring, Darius would go to Persepolis. There he would offer up his empire to his god, Ahura Mazda, and receive it back again. Bearded men from all parts of the empire would take gifts up the great stairway—camels, sheep, giraffes, humped bulls, and plates and cups of gold. The carvings on the stone buildings and stairway that show this were spectacular to look at. They were painted in gorgeous colors. The men's beards were made of bronze and lapis lazuli, and many figures wore crowns of real gold. Today, the gold is gone. No coloring is left, and the carvings are a dark gray.

The great stairway of Persepolis

Ahura Mazda and Zoroastrianism

Ahura Mazda is the name given to God by the religious teacher Zoroaster. According to tradition, he lived from about 628 B.C.E. to about 551 B.C.E.

Zoroaster taught that Ahura Mazda (above) was the only god and that he had created everything that was good in the world. Opposing him was a spirit named Ahriman (right), who had created everything that was evil. Ahura Mazda and Ahriman were constantly battling each other. People could show their support of Ahura Mazda by speaking the truth, helping the poor, and trying to make the world a better place in which to live. Anyone who was greedy, lazy, or proud was a supporter of Ahriman. Eventually Judgment Day would come. Then Ahura Mazda would triumph over Ahriman. The people who had supported Ahura Mazda would live happily ever after, while those who had supported Ahriman would suffer eternal punishment.

Zoroastrians consider fire a symbol of Ahura Mazda. That is why Zoroastrian temples keep a sacred fire burning at all times.

Most of Darius's reign was peaceful and prosperous. During the last years, however, trouble broke out along the empire's western borders. First, several Greek cities in Turkey revolted. Darius put down the revolt and then invaded the Greek mainland. To his dismay, the Persian army was soundly defeated at the battle of Marathon in 490 B.C.E. At this point, Egypt revolted as well. Furious, Darius prepared to punish both the Greeks and the Egyptians. However, he died in 486 B.C.E., before his army and navy were ready.

Xerxes

Darius's son Xerxes, who ruled the Persian Empire for twenty-one years, from 486 B.C.E. to 465 B.C.E., took up his father's dream of revenge. He decided to deal first with the Greeks. Accordingly, he assembled a fighting force of 200,000 men and led them to the Hellespont, a 1.5-mile-wide (2.4-km-wide) strait between Asia and Europe. There he poured a cup of wine into the water and recited a prayer for victory. Then he flung his sword into the strait and began building a bridge for his troops to use. (There were too many soldiers to transport them by sea.) The bridge was formed by lashing together some fifty wooden ships. The Persian army marched from the deck of one ship to the next all the way across the strait.

The king's prayer proved useless. Although the Persians won a victory on land, the Greeks won an even greater victory at sea. Xerxes had set up a throne on the shore of the bay of Salamis to see the Greeks defeated. Instead, he saw the newly built Greek fleet ram and destroy dozens of Persian ships.

Thousands of Persian sailors drowned because they did not know how to swim. Xerxes was forced to retreat, and the Persian Empire began to decline.

Alexander the Great

The man who finally overthrew the Achaemenid dynasty was one of the greatest conquerors the world has ever known. His name was Alexander, and he came from Macedonia, north of Greece. In 336 B.C.E., he led an army of Macedonian and Greek soldiers into southwest Asia. He was determined to take over the lands and wealth of the Persian Empire for himself.

And so he did. He began by defeating the Persians at Issus in what is now Turkey, in 333 B.C.E. Next he conquered Egypt. He defeated the Persians again at Arbela (also known as Gaugamela). When he reached Persepolis, he first removed all

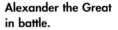
Alexander the Great in battle.

the books from its library and all the treasure from its palaces. Then he set fire to the city to show that *he*, not the Persian king, was the mightiest ruler in the world.

Like Cyrus before him, Alexander—once he achieved victory—was fair and generous. He employed thousands of Persians as government officials. He added additional thousands of Persians to his army. He even encouraged his Macedonian and Greek soldiers to marry Persian women by providing dowries for the brides!

The Seleucids

After Alexander died, in 323 B.C.E., three of his generals fought for power among themselves. Each general ended up with a kingdom of his own. Iran fell into the hands of Seleucus, who founded a dynasty that ruled the country for almost 100 years.

A great deal of international trade went on in those years. Goods moving between China and Europe passed through Iran. Iran itself exported carpets, precious stones, cotton, and such foodstuffs as lemons, melons, and sesame seeds.

Gradually, however, the Seleucids began to lose control over the different ethnic groups in their empire. By 250 B.C.E., the Seleucids were replaced as rulers of Iran by the Parthians.

The Parthians

The Parthians, who were related to the Persians, came from an area east of the Caspian Sea. They were superb warriors who fought on horseback. By 87 B.C.E., they ruled all the land between India and Greece. Over the next 300 or so years, they defeated the Romans repeatedly and kept the Roman Empire from expanding eastward.

In between fighting the Romans, the Parthians concentrated on two things: first, art, and second, trade with China. In art, they began to use a plaster finish called stucco on many of their buildings. They sculpted religious figures out of terra-cotta, a brownish orange clay, which was baked or fired. They covered their pottery with a beautiful green glaze. In trade, they opened diplomatic relations with China and introduced it to the cucumber and the onion. In return, China sent Iran the apricot and raw silk. The Parthians wove the silk thread into textiles that they exported to Europe.

Terra-cotta Parthian sculpture

The Parthians ruled most of Iran until 224 C.E. Then a purely Persian leader overthrew the Parthian dynasty. The new Persian Empire that the Sassanian dynasty created was even grander than the first.

The Mighty Sassanians

The founder of the Sassanian dynasty, which lasted for four centuries, was Ardashir I. He came from Pars in southern Iran and was an official at the Parthian court. Tradition says that, while he was there, he and the king's favorite wife fell in love,

The Sassanian Army

Sassanian armies boasted several new weapons. Elephants were used to frighten the enemy's cavalry horses. Chariots with scythes fastened to their wheels served to slash enemy foot soldiers. Weapons for attacking fortresses included catapults to hurl rocks over walls, and battering rams to knock walls down.

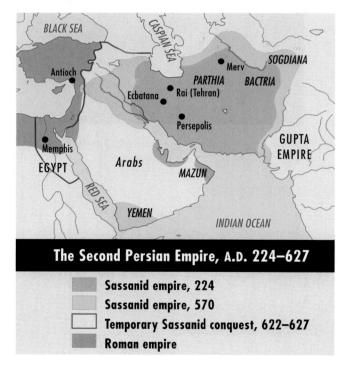

The Second Persian Empire, A.D. 224–627

- Sassanid empire, 224
- Sassanid empire, 570
- Temporary Sassanid conquest, 622–627
- Roman empire

and the two eloped. Ardashir then started a revolt against his former ruler. By 224, he had defeated the Parthians and became "King of Kings of the Aryans."

Ardashir was an excellent military leader who extended the borders of Iran eastward to India. He was also a wise ruler. Realizing that his military power depended on the taxes paid by farmers, he protected the farmers and treated them fairly. He also established Zoroastrianism as the national religion.

Ardashir was succeeded by his son Shapur I, who was an even better fighter than his father. In 260 he succeeded in capturing the Roman emperor Valerian. According to legend, he used the emperor as a mounting block, stepping on Valerian's back before getting on his horse.

Despite this legend, Shapur I was a highly educated man. He had scholars translate hundreds of books from Greek, Latin, and Sanskrit into the Persian language. The books covered such subjects as astronomy, medicine, and philosophy.

The third great Sassanian king was Chosroes I, who ruled Iran for forty-eight years, from 531 to 579. He is known as Chosroes the Blessed because he worked to improve his people's well-being. He restocked the empire's farms with cattle. He repaired its system of roads. He built new towns.

He reformed the tax system. He set up orphanages for children whose fathers had been killed in previous wars. He established scholarships to enable bright students who were poor to attend college. He provided dowries for poor women. He supported painters and other artists. He also tolerated religions other than Zoroastrianism, including Christianity.

Unfortunately for the Persians, most of Chosroes's successors did not follow his policy of caring for the people's welfare. Nobles spent most of their time either fighting or hunting. Also important were feasting for hours at a time and playing games imported from India, such as polo, tennis, and chess. Farmers grew poorer and poorer, yet taxes kept increasing. Peasant revolts became common. During one period of six years, seven different kings sat on the Persian throne. Finally, by 627, the Sassanian dynasty fell to new invaders: the Arabs.

The Arabs

The Arabs were a nomadic people from the deserts of Arabia, southwest of Iran. They are particularly significant in Iranian history because they brought with them the religion of Islam. Within 150 years or so, most Persians were Muslims. However, they followed the Shi'ite branch of Islam rather than the Sunni branch followed by most Arabs. You will learn about Islam's origin and beliefs and about the reasons for the Sunni-Shi'ite split in Chapter Eight.

Inspired by their religion, the Arabs soon conquered an empire that stretched from the Indus valley of India across

North Africa and into Spain. Gradually, however, the Arab Empire became more and more Persian. The Arabs stopped eating cross-legged on the ground and began eating at tables. Arab men wore Persian trousers instead of their traditional long robes. Arab soldiers learned how to use Persian catapults and battering rams. Arab rulers dressed like Sassanian kings and adopted the old Persian custom of having people bow to the ground before them. Persians filled many government posts, including that of vizier, or chief minister. The Arabs adopted the Persian postal system and the Persian coinage system. The coins even carried the old Persian design of two priests on either side of a Zoroastrian fire altar.

The Arabs ruled Iran for about 300 years. In the 900s, their control began to weaken, and several Persian provincial governors set up their own small kingdoms. Then, in the 1000s, a new group of invaders entered Iran, this time from the northeast.

The Turks

The original homeland of the Turks was central Asia. They conquered Iran on their way westward to their final home in present-day Turkey. They turned out to be mild rulers. So the Persians more or less governed themselves. They concentrated on scientific studies and on writing beautiful poetry. You will learn more about the great Persian poets of this period in Chapter Nine.

The Turks ruled Iran from 1040 to 1220. Then, like others before them, they were overthrown by new invaders.

The Mongols

The newcomers were the Mongols of eastern Asia. Their first invasion, in the 1220s, was led by Genghis (Chingis) Khan. Their second invasion, in 1256, was led by Genghis Khan's grandson, Hulagu Khan. Both invasions devastated Iran. Cities were leveled, qanats were destroyed, and tens of thousands of young Persian men were killed.

The Mongols used catapults to demolish the walls of Iranian cities.

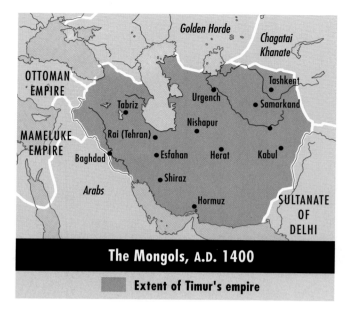

The Mongols, A.D. 1400

Extent of Timur's empire

Jalal ad-Din

Jalal ad-Din was the son of a Turkish king. He became a great hero in Persian literature because of the many battles he fought against the Mongol invaders. Although he lost every battle but one, he always managed a daring escape. Once, he reportedly rode his horse off a 50-foot- (15-m) high cliff into a river and then swam across it to safety.

In the 1380s, a third Mongol invasion took place. It was led by Tamerlane, or Timur the Lame. His rule had mixed effects on Iran. On the one hand, he destroyed several major cities. These included Esfahan, where he slaughtered 70,000 inhabitants and made a pyramid of their skulls. On the other hand, Tamerlane encouraged Persian architecture and miniature painting. He also placed many Persians in government positions.

After Tamerlane, Mongol power gradually fell away. In 1501, the third great Persian dynasty—the Safavid—gained the country's throne.

The Safavids

The founder of the Safavid dynasty was Ismail, who ruled for twenty-three years, from 1501 to 1524. He unified Iran and extended its borders. He also declared Shi'ite Islam the nation's official religion.

The greatest Safavid king was Shah Abbas the Great, who ruled for forty-one years, from 1587 to 1628. First he defeated several enemies. Then he spent the rest of his reign promoting religion, trade, and the arts.

Shah Abbas's greatest achievement was the completion of a new capital at Esfahan. In the city's center lay an immense, sand-covered square called the Royal Square. There, soldiers drilled, courtiers played polo, merchants sold their wares, and criminals were executed. Two mosques, or Muslim houses of worship, bordered the square. To the east stood a small mosque that Shah Abbas built for his father-in-law. To the south stood a larger mosque that Shah Abbas built for himself. Its blue-and-gold dome reflected light so brilliantly that at noon it shone like a second sun. A drum tower was located on the square's north end. There, every evening, an orchestra of drums and oboes played as the sun sank beneath the horizon. The custom was known as "drumming down the sun."

Outside the Royal Square, Esfahan was full of wide avenues and magnificent gardens. The city also contained a royal palace as well as numerous covered marketplaces called bazaars. Graceful arched bridges spanned the Zayandeh River. Esfahan was so beautiful that Persians began saying, "Esfahan nesf-e jahan"—Esfahan is half the world.

The Khaju Bridge, built by Shah Abbas, serves as a sluicegate that allows water to be stored behind it.

Nadir Shah

After the death of Shah Abbas, the Safavid dynasty faded from glory. For a brief time, Iran was ruled by the Afghans.

The Peacock Throne contains more than 20,000 precious gems, including diamonds, emeralds, and rubies.

Then a former slave and goat herder named Nadir Shah seized the Persian throne in 1736. He not only threw out the Afghans, he conquered Afghanistan itself. He then marched into India, where he won a smashing victory in just two months' time. Among the spoils he brought back to Iran were the Koh-i-noor diamond and the Peacock Throne. All Iran's shahs after Nadir Shah have been crowned while seated on the throne.

Although he was a military genius, Nadir Shah proved to be a cruel monarch. He was assassinated by his own bodyguards in 1747.

Following the death of Nadir Shah, Iran was divided into three kingdoms. Then, once again, a new dynasty arose: the Qajars.

The Qajars

The Qajar shahs ruled from 1794 to 1925. It was a difficult time for Iran. The nation faced two problems: new ideas and new enemies.

In those years, the sons of rich Iranian families went to college in Europe. When they returned home, they brought back information about the Industrial Revolution. By the twentieth century, they were also bringing back information about democracy and women's rights. This did not sit well with Iran's Islamic clergy and illiterate farmers. They wanted their country to stay unchanged.

At the same time, Iran attracted the interest of Russia and Great Britain. Russia was interested because most of its ports remain frozen for half the year. Control over Iran would enable Russia to gain access to the warm waters of the Caspian Sea and the Persian Gulf. Russia seized several Iranian provinces after fighting two wars, one in 1813, the second in 1828.

Great Britain was interested because it did not want Russian ships in the Persian Gulf to interfere with its trade route to India. At the time, Britain controlled most of India.

For their part, the Qajar rulers needed money. In exchange for cash, they granted concessions to both countries. For example, British financiers established the Imperial Bank of Persia. Russia, in turn, established its own bank. That meant that foreigners, rather than Iranians, issued the nation's banknotes. Both Russia and Britain opened mines and trading companies and tried to buy control of various industries, especially railroad construction and tobacco. They also organized military units of Iranians under the command of their own officers.

Things went from bad to worse. Iran's economy deteriorated as wealth from its natural resources left the country. The qanat system was breaking down, yet taxes on the farmers kept rising. Meanwhile, the shahs continued to spend lavishly on themselves and their families.

All these things greatly upset the Iranian people. By 1906 there was so much popular unrest that the ruling shah was forced to approve a constitution with an elected legislature. This marked the first change in Iran's 2,500-year tradition of absolute monarchy.

However, the legislators could not agree on a policy. Islamic clergy and merchants wanted to resist all foreign influence. Reformers wanted to use Westernization as a means to modernize and strengthen Iran. The result of the division between the two groups was a stalemate: Nothing happened.

In 1908 a significant event in Iran's modern history took place: the discovery of oil. In 1909 the Anglo-Persian Oil Company was formed to drill wells and build refineries along the Persian Gulf. Within a few years, oil had become Iran's main industry, and the Anglo-Persian Oil Company was the nation's biggest employer.

In the meantime, conditions in Iran grew more chaotic than ever. When World War I broke out in 1914, the country's sympathies lay with Germany, mostly because it opposed both Russia and Britain. Nevertheless, Iran declared itself neutral. Neither Russia nor Britain paid any attention to Iran's neutrality. Instead, they used Iran as a short cut for moving their troops to the war fronts.

World War I ended in November 1918. That winter, a severe famine hit Iran. Landlords and corrupt government officials hoarded food and sold it at inflated prices. Tens of

An early 1900 oil strike.

thousands of people starved to death. Russia withdrew from Iran, but Britain kept on trying to take over management of the country.

In 1923, the shah appointed a general named Reza Khan as his prime minister. The shah then left Iran to enjoy himself in France. It was a foolish act on his part. Two years later, Reza Khan seized the throne and set up a new dynasty: the Pahlavi.

Reza Khan Pahlavi

The new shah was determined to modernize Iran. He set about to change its social customs, economy, and government.

Instead of turbans and flowing pantaloons, men were now required to wear Western-style suits and hats. Women no longer had to wear the *chador*, a combination robe and veil that covers them from head to toe except for their faces and hands. The age at which they could be married was raised from nine to fifteen. Men had to tell their prospective brides whether they were already married and how many wives they had. (Islamic law allows a man to have up to four wives at the same time, provided he treats them all equally.) Muslim clerics lost much of their property and a great deal of their influence.

Reza Khan, founder of the Pahlavi dynasty

Reza Khan set up an Iranian bank in place of the British and Russian banks. He built Iran's first railroad. He also built cement, sugar, and textile mills, and founded the country's first university, the University of Tehran.

Reza Khan was backed by the army. As a result, he was able to more or less ignore the national legislature and determine policy by himself. He tried to bring the country's nomadic tribes under government control. Furthermore, he asked everyone to stop calling the country Persia. From then on, it was to be known only as Iran. Reza Khan wanted to emphasize the country's "pre-Islamic glory."

In 1939, World War II broke out. Once again, Russia—now known as the Soviet Union—and Britain were on one side, while Germany was on the other. Once again, Iran's sympathies lay with Germany. So in 1941, the Soviet Union and Britain occupied Iran. Three days later, Reza Khan abdicated, or gave up the throne. He then went to South Africa, where he died three years later.

Mohammad Reza Pahlavi

The Soviet Union and Britain decided that the new shah should be Reza Khan's oldest son, Mohammad Reza. He was a young man with a playboy reputation, and the two nations thought it would be easy to influence him.

In addition to the Soviet Union and Britain, Mohammad Reza had to deal with the United States. Some 30,000 American troops entered Iran to help move war supplies to the Russians. In 1943, American, British, and Russian leaders held a conference in Tehran.

Left to right: Soviet premier Josef Stalin, U.S. president Franklin D. Roosevelt, and British prime minister Winston Churchill at the Tehran Conference.

They agreed that their troops would be out of Iran within six months after the war's end.

World War II ended in 1945 and the United States and Britain kept their promise. The Soviet Union did not. Instead, it tried to force the shah to grant it oil concessions. It also encouraged separatist movements in the northern and western areas of Iran. The United States responded by giving the Soviet Union an ultimatum. Either all Russian troops were out of Iran in six weeks, or the United States would send in an army and make them leave. The Soviet Union withdrew. The separatist movements were crushed by the Iranian army.

Dr. Muhammad Mussadiq was in favor of a nationalized oil industry.

Several years later, in the early 1950s, another crisis erupted. An Iranian politician named Dr. Muhammad Mussadiq began making fiery speeches about the oil industry. The contract between Iran and the Anglo-Iranian Oil Company (formerly the Anglo-Persian Oil Company), he said, was unfair. It gave the British too large a share of the profits and left too little for Iran. Mussadiq wanted to nationalize the oil industry. That is, he wanted the Iranian government to operate the oil wells and refineries for itself and to keep the profits. Clerics, merchants, and students all supported Mussadiq—and the oil industry was nationalized in 1951.

Unfortunately, the government was unable to operate the oil wells and refineries properly. It did not have enough skilled technicians to replace the British technicians who left. Gradually, oil production dropped. Thousands of people lost their jobs and the government's income plummeted.

Finally, a civil war broke out between the forces of Mussadiq and those of the shah. The shah fled Iran, but four days later, with the backing of the United States, he returned, and Mussadiq was forced from office. The United States supported the shah because Iranian communists supported Mussadiq. The United States wanted to keep American oil interests in Iran out of the hands of groups sympathetic to the Soviet Union.

After Mohammad Reza Pahlavi returned to Iran, his power increased. Like his father, he wanted to modernize the country. He broke up large estates into small farms and gave them to the peasants. He built schools in rural areas. He set up a health care program that tackled such diseases as cholera, smallpox, and tuberculosis. He began planting trees on barren hillsides. He gave women the right to vote and to hold public office. Young men who were subject to the draft were allowed to teach or to serve as paramedics instead of entering the army. Hospitals went up in all the large cities. New roads spanned the country. The shah's reforms benefited the Iranian people as a whole. However, there were large pockets of discontent.

Although industrial production increased, agricultural production fell so much that the country had to import about one-third of its food. Thousands of farmers migrated to the towns, which did not have enough housing for them. Inflation was running at 40 percent per year.

The country's nomads were unhappy at being forced to give up their way of life. The clerics were unhappy about Westernization. It was against the laws of Islam, they said. In particular, it gave women too much freedom.

Many Iranians disapproved of the shah's lavish personal spending, especially when thousands of villages did not even have running water. Other Iranians wondered why so much money was going toward military equipment.

In addition, as time went on, the shah became more and more tyrannical. He limited free speech. He had people who criticized him either thrown in jail or exiled. He set up a secret police called the State Organization for Intelligence and Security (SAVAK) that spied on opponents and sometimes tortured them. He abolished all political parties except his own.

In spite of his efforts, however, the shah could not suppress opposition. Newspapers kept publishing articles criticizing his actions. Clerics preached against him. Workers went out on strike to protest his rule. More and more Iranians demonstrated in one city after another. They often clashed with the police, and hundreds of protesters were killed. Finally, by the end of 1978, it was clear that most Iranians wanted nothing more to do with Mohammad Reza Pahlavi.

On January 16, 1979, the shah fled Iran for the second—and last—time. Two weeks later, Ayatollah Khomeini returned to Iran from exile in France. He took control of the country on February 11, 1979.

The Khomeini Decade

Within a few months, Ayatollah Khomeini had set up a theocracy. You will learn about Iran's government in Chapter Five and about its society in Chapters Eight and Ten.

Khomeini's first years in power were chaotic. Hundreds of the shah's civil servants and military officers were put to death. Additional thousands were fired from their jobs. The new government banned political parties and shut down dozens of newspapers and magazines. Religious foundations took over the businesses and houses formerly owned by the royal family and wealthy industrialists. Many Westernized people such as doctors, nurses, teachers, and technicians fled the country. Even Abolhasan Bani-Sadir, the Islamic Republic's first president, left Iran for France.

Because the United States had supported the Pahlavi dynasty, the Islamic Republic was fiercely anti-American. In October 1979 the United States admitted Reza Shah Pahlavi for cancer treatments. The next month, Iranian students stormed the American embassy in Tehran and seized more than fifty people as hostages. The students demanded that the former shah be returned to Iran to stand trial. The United States refused.

The American embassy under siege in Tehran.

The students had originally planned to hold the embassy for only a week or so. Instead, Khomeini used the situation as a rallying point for his government. An American military mission to rescue the hostages failed, and eight American servicemen were killed. After 444 days in captivity, the hostages were finally released in January 1981.

In the meantime, the Islamic Republic faced external as well as internal problems. Since the early 1970s, disputes and border clashes between Iran and Iraq had been common. Iraq claimed ownership of Khuzestan, Iran's richest oil-producing province, as well as the Shatt-al-Arab. After the Islamic Revolution, Iran wanted to export the idea of theocracy to Iraq, which had a secular, or nonreligious, government.

Finally, in September 1980, Iraq invaded Iran. The resulting war lasted for eight years. Damage was severe on both

Above left: **Jubilant U.S. hostages return to freedom after 444 days in captivity.**

Above right: **Street fighting during the Iran-Iraq War.**

From Empire to Islamic Republic **61**

sides. Oil wells and refineries were bombed. About 5 million Iranians were made homeless. And at least 300,000 Iranian soldiers—some of them just eleven years old—were killed. Another 600,000 to 750,000 were wounded.

At last, in July 1988, Iran and Iraq agreed to a cease-fire. They have yet to sign an official peace treaty.

Mourners surround Khomeini's coffin during his funeral.

Since Khomeini

In 1989, Khomeini died. His funeral was the largest the world has ever seen. It is estimated that 2 million mourners attended the service. Only after several attempts was the hearse able to get to the cemetery through the crowds. People shoved and wept as they tried to rip off a piece of the shroud to keep as a holy relic. Hundreds of thousands of Iranians still visit Khomeni's shrine near Tehran each year.

Khomeini was succeeded as Iran's spiritual and political leader by Seyed Ali Khameini. Ali-Akbar Hashemi Rafsanjani was elected president in 1989 and reelected in 1993. A practical man, he tried hard to combat inflation and unemployment. He had only limited success.

In 1997 Seyed Mohammad Khatami became president. He was elected by an astounding 70 percent of the vote. A moderate cleric, Khatami pledged political and social reforms. These included a freer press, a more independent judiciary, and more opportunities for women and young people. In 2000, moderate reformers won a landslide victory in the election for the national legislature. Like Khatami, they obtained 70 percent of the vote.

Despite these two elections, government policy did not change. The conservative clerics who supervise the legislature vetoed most of the laws Khatami introduced. The conservative clerics who control the courts punished every behavior they considered un-Islamic. Censorship continued to be widely practiced. Dozens of proreform publications were shut down. Opposition leaders were thrown in jail, and some of them were murdered. Religious minorities were persecuted. Bloody student riots became common. Drug addiction spread, especially among the young.

In June 2001, Khatami was reelected president. This time he received a whopping 77 percent of the vote. In some places the turnout of voters was so heavy that the polls remained open an extra five hours, until midnight.

Khatami promised to continue pushing for more democracy and personal freedom in Iran. Yet questions remain. Will the country really be able to make reforms? Or will the conservative clerics who control the government continue to resist change? If political, social, and economic improvements are not made, what will the Iranian people do? Will they remain calm—or will they rise in revolt once again?

Only time will tell.

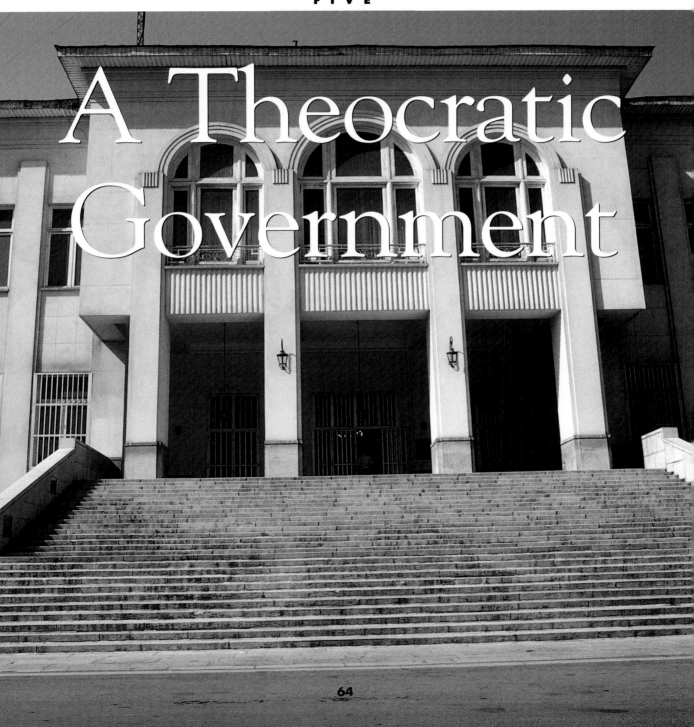

A Theocratic Government

I RAN'S OFFICIAL NAME IS THE ISLAMIC REPUBLIC OF IRAN. The name helps describe the country's government. It also shows one of the government's problems: how to combine religion and democracy.

Opposite: **The shah's palace in Tehran.**

Three Branches of Government

Iran adopted a new constitution in 1979. Like the constitution of the United States, it sets up three branches of government: executive, legislative, and judicial. Every Iranian age fifteen and older can vote in elections. The turnout is usually high. In 1997, for example, almost 80 percent of those eligible went to the polls.

The president is chosen every four years but can serve for only two terms. He is in charge of the day-to-day running of the country. He appoints cabinet members, supervises the economy, and carries out foreign policy. He must be a male cleric.

Iranians vote to choose a new parliament.

President Khatami

Seyed Mohammad Khatami was born in 1943, the son of a well-to-do cleric. After studying theology and philosophy, he served two years in the army. In 1978 he went to Germany to set up an Islamic center in the city of Hamburg. He returned to Iran in 1979 and became a member of the national legislature.

In 1982 Khatami was appointed minister of culture, a position he held for ten years. He was forced to resign in 1992 because he supported a filmmaker who had made a movie about the large number of casualties in the Iran-Iraq War.

After his resignation, Khatami became head of the National Library in Tehran. His election as president in 1997, in spite of clerical support for a different candidate, surprised everyone.

The legislature consists of a single house, called the Majlis. Like the president, members of the Majlis are elected every four years. Originally there were 270 members, but the number was recently raised to 290. The Majlis passes the country's laws.

The judicial system consists of the Supreme Court and a series of lower courts. The Supreme Court meets in Tehran; the lower courts, in various cities around the country.

Trials in Iran are very different from those in the United States. Most Iranian trials are held in secret, with no observers allowed. The judge, who must be a male cleric, also acts as the plaintiff, the prosecuting attorney, and the jury.

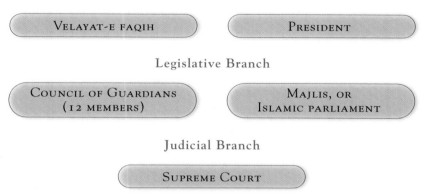

NATIONAL GOVERNMENT OF IRAN

Executive Branch

VELAYAT-E FAQIH

PRESIDENT

Legislative Branch

COUNCIL OF GUARDIANS
(12 MEMBERS)

MAJLIS, OR
ISLAMIC PARLIAMENT

Judicial Branch

SUPREME COURT

Iran's legal code is based on its interpretation of *sharia*, or Islamic law. In 1983 the code was revised to allow for certain traditional punishments that had been outlawed by the late shah. These include cutting off a person's hand for theft and stoning a person to death for adultery. In the case of murder, the criminal can be executed, not by the state, but by a member of the victim's family.

The Supreme Leader

Iran's constitution also created the position of *velayat-e faqih*, or "Islamic jurist." The velayat-e faqih, who is chosen for life, is the most powerful person in Iran. He is not only the country's spiritual leader but also its head of state. As such, he can overrule all other branches of government. For example, he can veto any decisions made by the president. He can declare war and make peace. If he disapproves of a bill the Majlis is

Tehran: Did You Know This?

Tehran is Iran's capital and largest city. It is also Iran's industrial center, home to three-fourths of the country's industries. It is a modern city, filled with block after block of high-rise apartment and office buildings. Only in the southern district, where poor people live, do you find one-story, dilapidated huts. Automobiles jam the streets, and a thick layer of smog blankets the city, especially in summer. A refreshing touch comes from the *jub*, or open-air canals, that run along many main streets. Residents have to be careful not to fall into the canals, though, for the jub overflow after the spring rains.

Tehran was founded in the 1000s. In the 1500s, a fortified wall and a citadel were built for protection. The city became Iran's capital in the late 1700s. In the early 1900s, most of the old wall was destroyed to make way for a grid of wide avenues. Today, Tehran sprawls over more than 240 square miles (600 sq km). Its main tourist attractions include the Azadi Tower and the National Jewels Museum, where you can see the gem-covered Peacock Throne.

Population (2002 est.): 10,000,000
Average Daily Temperature: 41°F (5°C) in January; 86°F (30°C) in July
Average Annual Rainfall: 12 inches (30.5 cm)

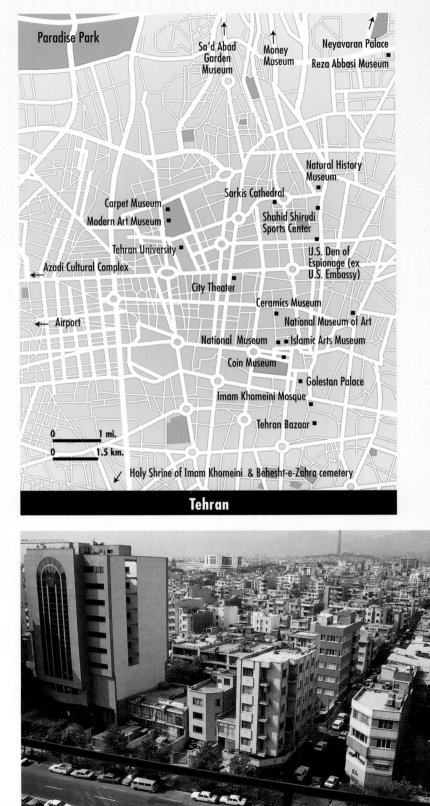

Tehran

considering, the bill is dead. He appoints the members of the Supreme Court and the head of the nation's radio and television systems. Lastly, he controls the army and the police.

The velayat-e faqih also chooses six of the twelve members of the Council of Guardians. (The other six are chosen by the judiciary.) It is the Council's responsibility to examine all laws, government actions, and court decisions to make sure that they do not violate the principles of Islam. The Council has the right to veto legislation. It can also reject candidates for the presidency and the Majlis.

Iran's first velayat-e faqih was Ayatollah Khomeini. Its second, and current, spiritual and political leader is Ayatollah Seyed Ali Khamenei. Iranians obeyed Khomeini without question

Ayatollah Khamenei

Seyed Ali Khamenei was born in 1939, the son of a poor cleric. He spent his early years studying and teaching Islam. In 1962 he began working with Khomeini to overthrow the shah. Khamenei was imprisoned for three years because of these activities. He was president of Iran from 1981 to 1989. He received the title of ayatollah soon after his election as velayat-e faqih.

because he had led the revolution against the shah and also because he was a widely respected scholar and teacher. Khamenei has less influence than Khomeini because his intellectual background is poorer, and he lacks widespread popular support.

Protecting the Country

Members of the Iranian military march in a parade celebrating Sacred Defense Week.

Iranian men are drafted for two years. (Recently, however, due to economic problems, the government has allowed draftees to pay a fee instead of having to serve.) They serve in the army,

The National Flag

Iran adopted a new flag in 1980. It contains three equal-sized horizontal stripes. From top to bottom, they are colored green, white, and red. The nation's emblem is centered in the middle of the white stripe. It is a double image of the word *Allah* (meaning God) in formal Arabic script. At the bottom of the green stripe and at the top of the red stripe is the phrase *Allah o Akbar*, or "God Is the Greatest," repeated eleven times in white.

the navy, or the air force. There is also a special armed group called the Revolutionary Guards. The Guards serve mostly as a police force.

In addition, groups of vigilantes (apparently financed by conservative clerics) have sometimes taken the law into their own hands. For example, during the 1980s they roamed the streets to make sure that women did not show any hair under their chadors. The vigilantes broke up private parties where they suspected that people had been drinking or dancing. In 1999, they invaded a student dormitory at the University of Tehran. Students who had protested against censorship were beaten. The vigilantes also stole the students' computers and refrigerators. Although the government condemned the invasion, it did not punish a single vigilante.

Earning a Living

I RAN'S LABOR FORCE IS EVENLY DIVIDED BETWEEN FARMERS and industrial workers. Although the country has abundant resources of oil and natural gas, it faces some serious economic problems.

Opposite: **Harvesting dates on a date palm plantation.**

A farmer irrigates his fields.

Farming and Herding

About 30 percent of Iran's working population are farmers. Some own and work small individual farms. Others are employed on large commercial farms. Due to lack of rainfall, only about 15 percent of the country's land can be cultivated. Even so, about half of the country's farmers rely on irrigation to grow their crops.

The leading cereal crops are wheat and barley. Other popular crops include rice, fruit, sugar beets, potatoes, nuts, tea, and tobacco. Both cotton and silk are becoming increasingly important.

Earning a Living **73**

Iran exports a large part of its pistachio production to the United States.

Iranian farmers work long and hard. In spite of their efforts, they cannot feed their country's fast-growing population. Iran has to import wheat, meat, chickens, eggs, and dozens of other farm products. Its leading farm export is nuts, especially the tasty pistachio.

Animal husbandry is practiced mostly by the nomads of western Iran. In summer they lead their flocks of sheep, goats, and camels up the high mountain slopes. In winter they descend to the milder valleys. The sheep and goats provide wool, meat, milk, and fat for cooking. The camels furnish wool and milk, and are also used for transportation. Some Iranians eat roasted camel humps and boil camel feet to make soup.

Sheep and goat herders tend their flocks.

What Iran Grows, Makes, and Mines

Agriculture

Wheat	8,700,000 metric tons
Sugar beets	5,500,000 metric tons
Tomatoes	3,500,000 metric tons

Manufacturing

Petroleum products	48,300,000 metric tons
Textiles, especially carpets	29,000,000 square meters
Cement	17,400,000 metric tons

Mining

Oil	3,400,000 barrels a day
Natural gas	80,000,000 cubic meters
Iron	6,000,000 metric tons

Weights and Measures

Iran uses the metric system.

Fishermen catch sturgeon in the mouths of the rivers flowing into the Caspian Sea.

Fishing

Iran's fishing industry, which is owned by the government, is centered in the Caspian Sea. There is some fishing in the Persian Gulf, but fisheries there were hurt by the Iran-Iraq War.

Sturgeon is the most important commercial fish. A single fish can weigh as much as 1 ton (454 kg)! Fishermen catch sturgeon in large nets, keeping the females but throwing the males back. Sturgeon supply both caviar and meat.

The oil industry is found mostly in the southwestern part of Iran.

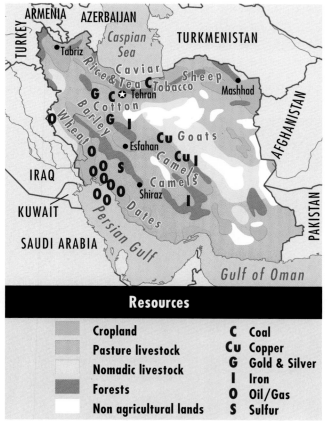

ARMENIA AZERBAIJAN
TURKEY
Tabriz
Caspian Sea
TURKMENISTAN
Rice & Tea
Caviar
Sheep
Mashhad
C Tobacco
G C Tehran
Cotton
G
O Barley
I
Wheat
Cu Goats
Esfahan
Cu I
Camels
O O O S Camels
O O O O Shiraz
Camels
O O Dates
I
IRAQ
KUWAIT
SAUDI ARABIA
Persian Gulf
Gulf of Oman
AFGHANISTAN
PAKISTAN

Resources

Cropland		C	Coal
Pasture livestock		Cu	Copper
Nomadic livestock		G	Gold & Silver
Forests		I	Iron
Non agricultural lands		O	Oil/Gas
		S	Sulfur

Industry

About 33 percent of Iran's working population is employed in industry. Most industries—including airlines, banks, insurance companies, oil, shipping, and utilities—are owned by the government.

Iran's leading industry is oil and natural gas. The country has about 10 percent of the world's oil reserves and the world's second largest reserves of gas. Oil makes up between 80 and 90 percent of Iran's exports.

Iran contains large deposits of coal, copper, gold, silver, sulfur, and iron ore. The country has some steel mills, as well as plants that produce automobiles, cement, fertilizer, sugar, and textiles.

The Bazaar

In addition to modern shopping malls and large department stores, Iranian cities contain traditional bazaars. These are covered mazes of stalls that are grouped according to what the merchants sell. For example, all the rug dealers are in one area and all the leatherworkers are in another area.

Bazaars are colorful places. They are filled with the aroma of flowers, spices, and food. Porters push carts piled with goods along the alleys. Boys carry trays of teapots and glasses. Men on motorcycles ride through, in spite of no-driving rules.

Prices in a bazaar are supposedly fixed, but merchants are happy to bargain. Some follow old ways of doing business, such as cutting fabric only on Mondays. All the merchants are men. As one Tehran merchant explained, "Women can shop, but they cannot sell."

Some bazaars also serve as a sort of community center. In addition to stalls, they contain mosques, meeting rooms, and public baths, which are similar to spas in the United States.

Bazaar merchants and clerics often work together politically. Neither group likes change. So the merchants give money to the mosques. In turn, the clerics pass laws that help the merchants.

Money Facts

Iran's unit of currency is the *rial*. Each rial equals 100 *dinars*, and 10 rials form 1 *toman*. As of January 20, 2002, a total of 1,755 rials was equal to U.S.$1.

The late shah encouraged tourism. Elegant hotels were constructed, especially along the Caspian Sea. Since the Islamic Revolution and the Iran-Iraq War, however, tourism has dwindled.

Transportation

Transportation within Iran is difficult because of the country's rugged terrain. About two-thirds of the roads are unpaved and better suited for donkeys and camels than for motorized transport. Nevertheless, there are two main corridors of transportation. One runs from Tehran south to the industrial centers and ports on the Persian Gulf. The other runs along the southern edge of the Caspian Sea.

Motorcycles are a common sight on busy city streets.

Iran's trains are fast, comfortable, and cheap. However, they do not run very often. Besides, Iran has only about 5,000 miles (8,046 km) of railroads. Most people get around by bus, truck, or car. However, if you travel in the northern part of Iran or near its borders with Pakistan and Afghanistan, you will encounter frequent roadblocks. This is partly a result of the Iran-Iraq War and partly to stop the smuggling of drugs from the east. In the large cities, many people ride around on motorcycles.

Ferries operate from port to port along the Caspian Sea. Persian Gulf ports handle most of Iran's trade, especially oil.

Domestic flights on the government-owned airline are frequent and reliable.

Communication

Iran's most popular means of communication is the radio. About four times as many people have radios in their homes as they do telephones or television sets.

Iran's telephone system, which is state-owned, is poor. Government offices receive priority service over private homes, and individual customers often wait for months before they get service. Breakdowns are frequent.

The Iranian government also owns the country's radio and television systems. It is against the law for these stations to broadcast anything that might be considered un-Islamic. However, many Iranians own illegal satellite dishes that enable them to watch CNN and other foreign TV stations.

In addition to owning the country's telephone, radio, and television facilities, the Islamic Republic licenses all newspapers and magazines. Under the press law of 1979, it has the right to close down any publication and to fine or imprison any writer or journalist who criticizes Islam or the government.

Iranians enjoy reading poetry and novels.

Customers purchase items in a well-stocked grocery store.

Iran does not look like a poor country. Customers fill its stores and restaurants. Supermarket shelves carry plenty of goods. There is little homelessness. People do not suffer from epidemics caused by bad water.

Nevertheless, Iran faces several economic problems. Its unemployment rate is at least 30 percent. Inflation is believed to run as high as 40 percent a year. Per capita income is lower now than it was at the start of the revolution. According to estimates, more than half the population now live below the poverty line.

One reason for Iran's economic problems is the fact that it relies so much on just one product: oil. Doing so makes the economy unstable. When oil prices are high, the country earns a great deal of money. Just after the revolution, oil was selling for U.S.$40 a barrel. During the 1990s, however, the price of oil plummeted to less than U.S.$10 a barrel. Tens of thousands of Iranians lost their jobs, and the government was forced to cut back on many of its activities.

Another reason for the country's economic difficulties is the system of *bonyads*, or foundations. The bonyads, which are owned by powerful clerics, are exempt from paying taxes and do not have their balance sheets audited. Yet somehow they manage to get almost all government contracts, even though they are inefficient. About 75 percent of Iran's businesses are run by the government.

Corruption, in fact, is widespread in Iran. You have to pay a bribe to get a business license or to import goods or raw materials. It is common practice for police officers to stop people on the street and ask for protection money. One result is that 85 percent of the population refuse to pay the income tax.

Sanctions, or economic penalties, that the United States imposed more than twenty years ago have also caused problems. When Iranians seized American hostages in 1979, the United States retaliated by taking over Iranian funds that had been invested or banked in the United States. It persuaded the World Bank and the International Monetary Fund not to make loans to Iran. The United States cut off all trade between the two nations. Recently, the United States loosened the sanctions a bit by agreeing to import Iranian carpets, caviar, dried fruit, and pistachios. Iran, however, would like to see the sanctions lifted completely.

A Varied Population

Because Iran lies near the crossroads of Europe and Asia, different peoples have always migrated there. Some simply passed through on their way to other lands. Some remained. In any event, the population in Iran today is a mixture of many ethnic groups.

About 51 percent of Iranians are Persians. They have always been the country's dominant nationality. The Persian language, Farsi, is Iran's official tongue. Most Iranians observe Persian customs and traditions. The country itself was known as Persia until 1934.

Ethnic Minorities

The largest minority group in Iran is the Azeris or Azerbaijani, who make up about 24 percent of the population. They are concentrated in the northwestern part of the country. Although related to the Turks, they speak their own language, Azeri. They work mostly as herders, farmers, and merchants.

The Mazandarani make up about 8 percent of the population. They live in a long valley that runs from Tehran to the Caspian Sea. They speak a dialect of Farsi and earn a living mostly as fishermen and farmers.

The third largest minority group is the Kurds, who make up about 7 percent of the population. They live in the northern part of the Zagros Mountains and speak Kurdish (or Kordi). There are also Kurds in Turkey, Iraq, and Syria.

Opposite: **Today, Iran has a diversified population.**

From Farsi to English

English has borrowed more than 150 words from Farsi. Among them are the following:

bazaar
caravan
khaki
lemon
lime
magic
margarine
pajama
paradise
peach
rice
scarlet
spinach
tiger
tulip

Turkish Kurds live on the Iranian border.

Ethnic Breakdown in National Population

Persians	51%
Azeris (Azerbaijani)	24%
Mazandarani	8%
Kurds	7%
Arabs	3%
Baluchis	2%
Turkmen (Turkomani)	2%
Luri (Lors)	2%
Other minorities	1%

A nomadic herding people, the Kurds have wandered across the borders of all four countries for centuries. After World War I, they tried to form a nation of their own, but without success. Many Iranian Kurds were moved from one region of the country to another by the late shah, whose government they opposed. During the 1970s, he deported about 100,000 of them to Iraq.

The remaining ethnic groups of Iran are much smaller. The Arabs make up about 3 percent of the population. They speak a dialect of Arabic. They live mostly in the province of

Khuzestan in Iran's southwest and work in the oil industry there. Because they have close family ties with people in Iraq, many of them would like to see Khuzestan become part of that country. This was one of the reasons for the Iran-Iraq War.

The Baluchis make up about 2 percent of the population. They live in the southeastern part of Iran and speak a language related to Farsi. Former nomads, they are now mostly farmers. They are famous for their camel races.

The Turkmen, or Turkomani, likewise make up about 2 percent of the population. They are concentrated in northeastern Iran. They speak their own language, Turkmen, and follow the Sunni branch of Islam. In the past, they were known as fierce warriors, but today they are mostly farmers and fishermen. They raise the best horses in Iran.

Major Languages

Altaic Languages
Turkic (Turkmen, Turkish, Azeri)
Indo-European Languages
Iranian (Persian, Luri, Mazandarani)
Iranian (Kurdish)
Other
Semitic Languages
Arab
Sparsely Inhabited

Several tribes inhabit the central and southern parts of the Zagros Mountains. The Luri (or Lors) make up about 2 percent of the population. They speak either their own language, called Luri, or a dialect of Arabic. The Baktiari are related to the Luri and speak the Luri language. The Qashqai speak Turkish.

The Arabic Script

When the Arabs first came to Iran in the 600s, they brought not only Islam but also their language and their script. Although many Arabic words made their way into the Persian language, the Iranians basically kept their own tongue. However, they began writing it in the Arabic script.

Iranians still use the Arabic script today. It is written from right to left and has twenty-eight symbols for the letters, or sounds, of the alphabet. Its graceful forms are often used to decorate dishes, buildings, and books.

In the past these tribes were nomadic. During the 1960s, the shah tried to force them to abandon their way of life and settle in farming villages. The Islamic Republic has done the same. No one really knows how many of these tribes remain nomadic.

Some Farsi Phrases

Salam	Hello
Khoda hafez	Goodbye
Hale shoma chetor-e?	How are you?
Kheili mamnun.	Thank you very much.
Khakesh me konam.	You're welcome.
Lotfan	Please
Babakhshid.	Excuse me.
Shoma engelisi baladid?	Do you speak English?

Refugees

At the present time, Iran is host to more refugees than almost any other country in the world. Many are Kurds fleeing persecution in Turkey or Iraq. The majority are Afghans, who number between 1.5 and 2.3 million.

The Afghans poured across the border during the 1970s and 1980s to escape both the Soviet invasion of their country and, later, Afghanistan's civil war. Many Iranians blame them for all sorts of domestic problems, ranging from unemployment to unsolved murder cases. In recent years the Iranian government has tried to send Afghan refugees back, but without much success.

In the first half of 2001, a new stream of Afghan refugees began arriving in Iran. They were fleeing a famine caused by three years of drought. After the September 11 terrorist attacks on New York City and Washington, D.C., thousands of additional Afghans tried to enter Iran. They wanted to avoid the American bombing of Afghanistan. Although Iran closed the border, many Afghans probably were able to make the crossing.

One of many Afghan families at the Shahid Arbabi refugee camp in Iran in October 2001.

Population of Major Cities

Tehran (2002 est.)	10,000,000
Mashhad	1,887,405
Esfahan	1,266,072
Tabriz	1,191,043
Shiraz	1,053,025

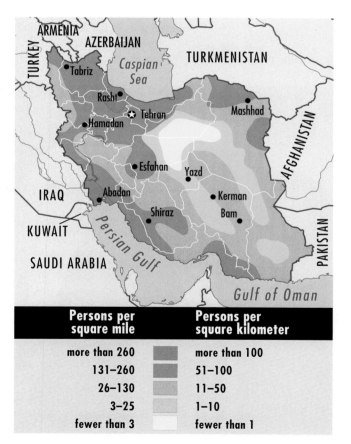

Persons per square mile		Persons per square kilometer
more than 260		more than 100
131–260		51–100
26–130		11–50
3–25		1–10
fewer than 3		fewer than 1

From Countryside to City

Over the last several decades, more and more Iranians have left the countryside and moved to urban areas. At present about 60 percent of the people live in cities, and their number keeps going up all the time. About one-quarter have squeezed into Tehran, which is by far the nation's largest city. Other sizable cities include Esfahan, Mashhad, Shiraz, and Tabriz.

Iran's cities are a combination of old and new. Narrow, twisting streets, many without names, often occupy the city's center. Surrounding this old section are wide thoroughfares and high-rise buildings. There are separate areas for businesses, houses, and government offices. Traffic is usually ferocious. Traffic lights are few and far between, and people are killed in automobile accidents almost every day. The sewage systems are not adequate. Most buildings depend on individual septic tanks.

In both city and countryside, the most important social group is the extended family. In addition to parents and children, it includes uncles, aunts, and cousins. Members of an extended family usually live close to one another. Sometimes they even share the same house. They socialize

together and help one another out when needed. Family members always try to eat together. In the city, working fathers often go home for a two-hour lunch break.

Iranians, in general, are extremely sociable. They love to entertain family and friends in their homes. The men also

The extended family gives Iranians both security and sociability.

A smoking garden is the perfect place to sit and chat while smoking a "hubble-bubble" pipe.

spend considerable time in teahouses, sitting, talking, and smoking "hubble-bubble pipes." (Water in the pipes cools the tobacco smoke before it is inhaled.)

A Population Explosion

The total population of Iran is now somewhere between 66 and 75 million. At the time of the Islamic Revolution, it stood at less than 40 million. Ayatollah Khomeini encouraged families to have children. He felt that large numbers of Iranians would help spread the ideas of the Islamic Revolution. Also, soldiers were needed for the war against Iraq.

The population explosion has created numerous economic problems. Iranian industries and businesses are unable to provide jobs for all the people who are looking for work. The country also suffers from a serious housing shortage, as well as growing shortages of food and water.

In recent years, the Islamic Republic reversed its policy and is now encouraging population control. However, it is a country of the very young. Only 4 percent of the people are older than sixty-five. About half are under the age of twenty. That means that the population will continue to increase for several decades to come.

The average number for an Iranian family is six.

Islam in Iran

ISLAM IS THE YOUNGEST AND FASTEST-GROWING OF THE world's three major monotheistic (the belief in one God) religions. Most Iranians belong to the minority Shi'ite branch of Islam. However, their beliefs and religious holidays closely resemble those of the majority Sunnis.

Opposite: **Dome and minaret in Esfahan**

The Prophet of Allah

Islam's founder was an Arab named Muhammad. He was born around 570 in the city of Mecca in what is now Saudi Arabia. In those years, Mecca was a center of international trade. It was also a religious center. Arab pilgrims gathered there once a year to worship at a black stone that they believed had fallen from paradise.

Muhammad became a wealthy merchant. He did not like the drinking and gambling he saw around him, especially since they often led to bloodshed. He also wondered about the religious beliefs of the Jewish and Christian traders he met in Mecca. They worshiped a single God, while the Arabs worshiped many gods.

Muhammad began to think about the nature of God and the way people ought to behave. In 610 he had a revelation. An angel, Gabriel, appeared and ordered him to recite a message in the name of God. After three years of hesitation, Muhammad finally recited the message.

The message that Muhammad recited was that there is only one true god—Allah, or *The* God. All believers in Allah are equal. The rich should help the poor. People should not collect interest on loans. Nor should they gamble, drink liquor, or eat pork. These rules from God were later written down in Islam's holy book, the Qur'an (also spelled Koran).

Gradually more and more people adopted the new religion. However, the leaders of Mecca were unhappy. They believed their city's economy would be ruined because pilgrims would no longer come there. They were also afraid that Muhammad was becoming too powerful politically. So they began to attack Muslims. Finally, in 622, Muhammad and his followers left Mecca and went to the city of Yathrib, known today as Medina. This journey became known as the *hejira*, or flight. The year 622 became the first year of the Islamic calendar.

Muhammad turned out to be an excellent military and political leader. In Medina he organized an army that defeated a much larger Meccan army. In 630, he went on to conquer Mecca itself. There he dedicated the *Kaaba*, the building that housed the black stone, to the worship of God and made Mecca Islam's center. Soon after, 100 tribes from all over Arabia converted to Islam and swore allegiance to Muhammad. They then set out to conquer and convert other peoples.

Muhammad and his followers on their journey to Medina.

The Sunni-Shi'ite Split

Muhammad died in 632. Unfortunately, he did not name anyone to succeed him as the religious and political head of Islam. He did not even set up a system for choosing a successor. A dispute over leadership arose at once.

Some Muslims argued that the leader should be related to Muhammad. They supported his son-in-law Ali. Other Muslims disagreed. They argued that the leader should be chosen in the traditional way, namely, through agreement by the community's elders.

Ali was eventually chosen as leader of the Islamic community. After five years in office, he was assassinated, and a man named Mu'awiyah became the leader. Mu'awiyah founded the Umyyad dynasty, which expanded the borders of the Arab Empire from India to Spain. His followers became known as Sunnis.

In the meantime, Ali's son Hussein took over the claim of succession. Iranians supported him because he had married a daughter of the last Sassanian king. Hussein's followers became known as Shi'ites.

In 680, Hussein and 72 of his supporters were attacked by a Sunni army of 4,000 men at the town of Karbala in what is now Iraq. Hussein was stabbed to death while holding a sword in one hand and the Qur'an in the other. His martyrdom made the split between Sunnis and Shi'ites permanent. To Shi'ites, the battle of Karbala symbolizes the struggle between good and evil.

As the years went on, other differences between Sunnis and Shi'ites developed. However, the original dispute over succession remains the most important disagreement.

Sufism

Sufism is a mystical movement within Islam that emphasizes the love of Allah and humanity. Sufis practice poverty and nonviolence. They do not consider religious ritual particularly important. During the 1100s and 1200s, many Persian Sufis wrote poems describing how people could become closer to God.

Shi'ite Muslims have five "pillars of faith," or religious duties that they are required to perform.

The first pillar of faith is to declare one's religious belief by saying: "There is no God but God, and Muhammad is the messenger of God."

The second pillar is to pray three times a day. (Sunni Muslims pray five times daily.) Six days a week, Shi'ites pray wherever they happen to be. On Friday, the Muslim sabbath, they usually pray in a mosque. Prayers are said in Arabic, which is the language of the Qur'an. People face in the direction of Mecca while praying.

The third religious duty is to give money to the poor. Muslims are supposed to give one-fortieth of their income.

The fourth religious duty is to fast during the daylight hours of the month of Ramadan.

Students at Tehran University bow toward Mecca at Friday prayers.

The fifth pillar is *hajj*, or pilgrimage to Mecca. Every Muslim who is healthy enough and wealthy enough is supposed to make the hajj once in a lifetime if he or she can. The hajj takes place during the last month of the Muslim year.

Male pilgrims wrap themselves in white cloth before entering Mecca.

The Shi'ite Clergy

Shi'ite Islam does not have a formal priesthood. However, it has always had learned men who interpret the Qur'an and other religious works. In Iran such men are called *mujtahids*, or "jurists." One becomes a mujtahid by taking courses at a *madreseh*, or religious college, and by passing exams.

The highest rank of a mujtahid is that of *ayatollah*, or "sign of God." An ayatollah is something like a Supreme Court justice with a Ph.D. degree in religion. An ayatollah receives his rank from other clerics. He is expected to be well educated, to have taught many students, and to have written many books. The more disciples he has, the greater his influence. Iran usually boasts five ayatollahs at any one time.

The next highest rank is that of *hojatolislam*, or "proof of Islam." Mullahs make up the lowest rank. They are the least educated of the mujtahids, having studied only one or two years.

Religious Holidays

The month of Ramadan—the ninth month of the Muslim year—is considered sacred. It is the month in which Muhammad was born, received his revelation, made the hejira, and died.

During Ramadan, Muslims carry on their usual activities. However, they do not eat or drink between sunrise and sunset. There are several exceptions, though, including pregnant women and those who are sick or elderly. Fasting is supposed to focus people's attention on God. It is also thought to make them more compassionate toward the poor.

Ramadan ends the night a new moon appears in the sky. Cannons boom in celebration, and families sit down to a special feast. Among the delicacies served are chicken sautéed with onions and eggplant, lamb stuffed with dried fruit, and sugar candies and pastries.

The timing of Ramadan shifts from year to year. Sometimes it comes in winter and sometimes in summer. That is because the Islamic calendar follows the 28-day cycle of the moon rather than the 365-day cycle of the sun.

Pilgrimage to Mashhad

Each year, hundreds of thousands of pilgrims make their way to the city of Mashhad in northeastern Iran. Mashhad is the nation's holiest city. It houses the tomb of Imam Reza, the only *imam*, or spiritual leader, who is buried in Iran. After invaders destroyed the original tomb, Shah Abbas the Great ordered construction of the present tomb (pictured). It is covered with a gold dome. Blue tiles decorate the walls and fountains bubble in the courtyard. Inside, Imam Reza's body rests behind a golden gate. Non-Muslims may walk quickly across the courtyard, but they are forbidden to enter the holy shrine itself.

Men parade carrying a picture of Hussein during the religious holiday of Ashura.

The religious holiday of Ashura marks the anniversary of Hussein's death at Karbala. For two days, men wearing black shirts parade through city and village streets. They carry flags, weapons, and pictures of the martyr. As they walk, they wail aloud and hit themselves on their backs and chests to show their sorrow. Groups of actors put on passion plays called *ta'ziyeh*, or "mourning for Hussein." The actors portraying Hussein and his followers usually wear green. The actors portraying the Sunni killers are usually dressed in red.

Religions of Iran

Muslim	99%
Christian	0.3%
Jewish	0.07%
Zoroastrian	0.03%
Bahai	0.6%

Religious Minorities

Although about 99 percent of its population is Muslim, Iran contains several religious minorities. These include Christians, Jews, Zoroastrians, and Bahai.

Christians number about 200,000. Most are Armenians who came to Iran in the early 1600s. They are concentrated in Tehran, where they are active in business and trade. They speak Armenian, publish their own newspaper, and run their own schools.

Jews have lived in Iran for more than 2,500 years. For most of that time, they were part of the life of the country. Since the Islamic Revolution, however, things have changed. All Jewish newspapers have been closed, and Jews are not allowed to speak Hebrew or run their own schools. As a result, their numbers have dwindled from about 80,000 to about 30,000. At present, they live mostly in the cities of Tehran, Esfahan, and Shiraz. Many work in the jewelry business and in the bazaars.

Although longtime residents of Iran, Jews account for a very small percent of the population.

Although Zoroastrianism was the official religion before the coming of Islam, fewer than 10,000 Zoroastrians remain in Iran. Most live in the cities of Kerman and Yazd. (About 170,000 Zoroastrians, whose ancestors migrated from Iran in the 700s, live in India, where they are known as Parsis.)

The Bahai religion, developed in the mid-1840s, is an offshoot of Islam. The government does not allow the Bahai to practice their faith. Although they pay taxes and the men serve in the army, they cannot vote or attend a university. The state does not even recognize their marriages. Despite all this, about 350,000 Bahai still remain in Iran.

A Vibrant
Culture

I RANIANS HAVE MADE MANY CONTRIBUTIONS IN SUCH FIELDS as architecture, poetry, and miniature painting. Persian carpets are the most highly prized in the world. Iranian movies are seen and admired everywhere.

Opposite: **Detail in this carpet shows a wildlife theme.**

Architecture

Before the coming of Islam, Persian architecture focused on palaces. They were usually made of stone, with paintings and sculptures adorning the walls. After the coming of Islam, the emphasis shifted to mosques, and stone was replaced by oven-baked or sun-dried brick. Architects created a decorative effect by laying the bricks in zigzag patterns or by using bricks of different sizes.

Decorative brickwork was used on the tower of the Citadel of Karim Khan.

Most mosques in Iran today are noted for their beautiful tile-covered domes. The tiles are mostly blue and white, but other colors— such as pink, olive green, yellow, and brown—are also used.

Beautiful tile work decorates the dome and minarets of this mosque.

In addition to a central dome, each mosque has one or more minarets, or towers. The muezzin, who calls people to prayer, stands on a walkway that goes around the minaret just below its pointed top. In recent years, many muezzins have been replaced by records broadcast through loudspeakers.

Poetry

Iranians take their poetry very seriously. They love to memorize and recite poems. Many shahs hired poets to live and write at the court. Many streets and squares are named after poets.

The first of the great Persian poets was Ferdosi. He was born around 940 and spent more than thirty years of his life writing the *Shahnameh*, or *The Book of Kings*. Iranians consider this stirring poem their national epic. It contains accounts of the fifty heroic kings who supposedly ruled Iran from the creation of the world down to the Arab conquest.

The second great Persian poet was Omar Khayyám (about 1047–about 1123). Before he began writing poetry, he worked as an astronomer and a mathematician. Khayyám's major poem is the *Rubaiyat*. It contains about 1,000 four-line poems, many of them rather sad.

Yet another great poet was Saadi (about 1207–about 1291), sometimes called the "Shakespeare of Iran." He won fame for *Golestan*, or *The Rose Garden*. This work has nothing to do with roses. Rather, it contains stories about kings and ordinary people. Most of the stories teach a moral.

Iran's fourth famous poet was Hafiz (about 1324–1389). He wrote some 700 lyrical poems about love, religion, and human behavior. Many Iranians still use his collected works as an oracle. They say a special prayer to Hafiz. Then they open the book at random and read the first line of the poem at the top of the right-hand page. If interpreted properly, the line supposedly predicts the future or tells the reader what to do.

Iran's greatest modern poet was probably Ahmad Shamlu (1925–2000). Many of his works deal with political freedom. They were banned by both the shah and the Islamic Republic.

An artist works on a miniature painting.

Persian Miniatures

Iranian artists developed the technique of miniature painting after the coming of Islam. According to traditional Islamic practice, artists are not supposed to show the human form or face. In miniature painting, however, the figures are so small that they cannot possibly be confused with pictures of real people. Furthermore, artists use miniature paintings to illustrate only secular subjects, such as hunting scenes, fairy tales and legends, and scenes of life at court. Religious scenes are never shown. Therefore, no one can accuse the artists of breaking Islamic law.

Miniatures are painted in brilliant colors, often against a gold background. Iran's most famous miniatures date from the 1400s and 1500s.

The Cinema

Iran is now the tenth largest producer of films in the world. About one-third are made by the government, the rest by individual filmmakers. Filmmaking is a popular profession for young people. They produce very imaginative films in spite of poor equipment and government censorship.

Iranian films usually deal with the theme of good against evil. Some are slapstick comedies or violent action films. Others are quieter and more thoughtful. They tend to use amateur actors, often children, and are frequently set outdoors. Several have won international awards.

One of the country's leading film directors is Abbas Kiarostami, who directed such films as *Taste of Cherry* and *The Wind Will Carry Us*. *Taste of Cherry* has not been shown in Iran because it deals with suicide, a subject that is taboo in Islam. *The Wind Will Carry Us* depicts the experiences of an engineer who comes to a small mountain village.

Two of Kiarostami's former assistants have gone on to become well-known directors themselves. Bahman Ghobadi recently directed *A Time for Drunken Horses*. In this film, a teenage boy becomes a smuggler in order to earn money for an operation that will keep his younger brother alive. Jafar Panahi's *The White Balloon* is a delightful film that shows Tehran's street life through the eyes of a seven-year-old girl. His film *The Circle* has been banned by Iranian authorities because it portrays some of the difficulties that women face in the Islamic Republic.

Surprisingly, Iran's biggest box office hit in recent years was the film *Two Women*. Made by a woman director, Tahmineh Milani, it tells the story of two women who met in college years before. One is happily married. The other is not. Her husband forbids her to continue her studies or to read books. He even locks up the telephone. When she seeks a divorce, the judge refuses her. After all, he says, her husband does not gamble, beat her, or stay out all night. Then her husband is killed—and she wonders how she will manage. "I feel like a free bird but I don't have wings to fly," she says. "I must work, go to school, be the father and mother to my children."

Director Milani said that the two women are really different views of the same person. The happy woman is how Islamic society sees her. The unhappy woman is how she sees herself.

Music

Music has always been part of Iranian life. Strolling musicians entertained at the courts of the shahs. Villagers played music at weddings.

Present-day Iranian music usually revolves around Islam. Most of it is soothing to listen to and some of it is rather sad.

Googoosh

During the 1970s, Iran's leading pop diva was Faegheh Atashnin, better known as Googoosh. She was a magnificent singer who specialized in romantic songs that combined traditional Iranian music with Western musical styles. Her fans idolized her. If she changed her haircut or her clothing style, they changed theirs too.

Then came the Islamic Revolution. Pop music was banned. Women singers were not allowed to perform for audiences that included men. Music stores could not display CDs and cassettes of female performers.

Googoosh went into retirement. After being retired for more than twenty years, she received permission in 2000 from the Iranian government to tour abroad. Her

concerts in Canada and the United States (both of which have large groups of Iranian exiles) drew tens of thousands of listeners. They cheered and wept as Googoosh performed.

Iranians play a variety of musical instruments. The *sitar* is a three-stringed instrument similar to a guitar. The *oud* has six to thirteen pairs of strings. Some musicians like an instrument resembling an oboe. There are different kinds of drums and horns. There is even a type of bagpipe.

Every April, Tehran hosts an Iranian Epic Music Festival in which participants sing about the glories of ancient Persia. Most of these epic songs go on for hours.

Persian Carpets

Iranians have been weaving carpets for more than 2,500 years. It is probably their most famous art form.

Persian carpets have many different colors and designs, depending on where they are made and who makes them. For example, Kurdish carpets often show animals. Baktiari carpets show flowers and vines. A carpet made in Na'in will probably be colored blue and beige. One made in Tabriz will contain red.

Most Persian carpets are made from either wool or silk. The best dyes come from natural sources such as herbs, plants, and the skins of fruit and vegetables. In recent years, chemical dyes have become more popular. Each dye color has a meaning. For example, orange represents faith in God. Red stands for wealth or happiness.

Weaving a carpet by hand is very slow work. It may take an entire year to make a 9-foot (2.75-m) by 12-foot (3.66-m) carpet. Machine looms are much faster, but machine-made carpets do not have the charm and character of a good handmade carpet.

Iranians use carpets for many purposes besides covering floors. They kneel on carpets when they say their prayers. They hang carpets on their walls. Nomads use carpets as doors for their tents. A carpet often indicates how wealthy a family is. Carpets even serve as a form of currency.

A 9-foot by 12-foot carpet contains more than 7 million knots.

Lifestyles

T
HE DAILY LIFE OF IRANIANS IS SHAPED TO A GREAT EXTENT
by Islam. The religion influences the way people dress,
the education they receive, their marriage customs, and even
their sports.

Opposite: **In Iran, female students receive the same level of education as male students.**

Eating Well

Iranian cooking is based on rice. Iranians eat it either plain or
covered with a sauce made from meat and vegetables. The
country's national dish, the *chelo kebab*, is rice with a kebab on
top. The kebab consists of pieces of marinated lamb that have
been threaded onto a metal skewer—usually with onions and
tomatoes—and broiled over charcoal.

Lamb kebabs with two types of rice

People wait in line for freshly baked bread at the neighborhood bakery.

The second staple of Iranian cooking is unleavened bread, which is bread made without yeast. People bake their own bread in the villages. In the cities, they buy it at neighborhood bakeries.

Iranians combine a large helping of rice or bread with many small side dishes. Popular side dishes include radishes, eggplant, spinach, chickpeas, cucumber, raw onions, and eggs. A bowl of yogurt accompanies most meals.

Iranians are very fond of soups. The one most often eaten by far is barley soup, but people also make soup from pomegranates, dried fruit, and yogurt.

The favorite meat is lamb. Islam forbids the eating of pork, and Iranians seldom have beef because pastureland is scarce. Fish is readily available along the northern and southern coasts.

The best-known fruit is the sweet Persian melon. Other fruit include apples, cherries, grapefruit, kumquats, peaches, plums, and watermelon. Nuts include almonds, hazelnuts, walnuts, and especially pistachios.

Iranians have a decided sweet tooth. They are especially fond of a honey-and-nut pastry called baklava and a candy called halva, made of sesame seeds and honey.

A vendor chooses a ripe watermelon for these women.

Baking *Non-e Shirini* Cookies

1. Preheat the oven to 350°F (176.6°C).
2. Beat 5 egg whites in a mixing bowl until they foam. Slowly add 1 cup of sugar and beat until the egg whites become stiff.
3. Add 1 tablespoon of grated orange rind and 2 tablespoons of lemon juice, and mix thoroughly.
4. Add 1 cup of chopped walnuts and mix thoroughly.
5. Drop spoonfuls of the batter onto a greased cookie sheet.
6. Bake until the cookies are golden brown.

A waiter serves tea to customers at a restaurant in Tehran.

At one time Iranians drank Turkish coffee. Nowadays, however—except among the Armenians—the national drink is tea. It is served scalding hot in a small glass cup without a handle. Instead of putting a sugar cube in the cup, you hold it in your mouth between your teeth. The cube dissolves slowly as you sip the tea.

Clothing

Most Iranian men wear full, loose trousers and either long-sleeved or short-sleeved shirts without ties. Shorts are permitted only for swimming or playing an official sport. Clerics wear a full-length black or brown robe. If they are descended from the Prophet Muhammad they wear black turbans. Otherwise they wear white turbans.

Men in traditional Iranian dress

Iranian women are required to wear proper Islamic dress when they leave home. Most women wear black chadors with socks or thick tights. At home, women may dress as they please. Rich Iranian women follow the latest fashions from Paris and Milan.

Wearing a chador is uncomfortable in hot weather.

This Turkoman proudly wears his distinctive hat.

Some of Iran's ethnic minorities have kept their traditional clothing. For example, you can tell a Turkoman man by his huge sheepskin hat, which he wears even in the summer. You can tell a Turkoman woman by her ankle-length silk dress of red or maroon.

Perhaps the most colorful clothing style is that of the Kurds. A Kurdish man wears baggy pants and an embroidered shirt. He ties a wide sash around the shirt and sticks a dagger in the sash. He puts an embroidered skullcap on his head and tops it with a turban. In the past, Kurdish men wore sandals on their feet, but nowadays they usually wear sneakers.

These Kurdish women wear long, pleated dresses.

A Kurdish woman wears satin pants and a pleated slip, over which she puts several long cotton dresses, one on top of the other. The dresses have zippers down the front and big safety pins at the neck. Kurds believe that the zippers and pins protect them from evil spirits that attack in the night.

Housing

Iranian cities contain modern, high-rise apartment buildings made of steel and glass. Small shops line the pavements at ground level. Private homes are often built around a closed courtyard that usually contains a garden and a pool.

Houses in villages along the Caspian Sea are made of wood and are two stories high. Elsewhere in the country, village houses are only one story high. They are made of mud bricks, which are cheap and plentiful. The bricks help to keep the houses warm in winter and cool in summer.

Houses in mountain villages have no windows. They use a roof hole for light and ventilation. Houses in plateau villages have high walls with flat straw roofs on which people often store provisions. Plateau villages center around a square that contains a mosque and a public bath. Surrounding each village is a clay wall that helps to protect the inhabitants from winds, sandstorms, and bandits. Most villages lack electricity and running water. People get their light from oil lamps and their water from a common well.

A home in a plateau village

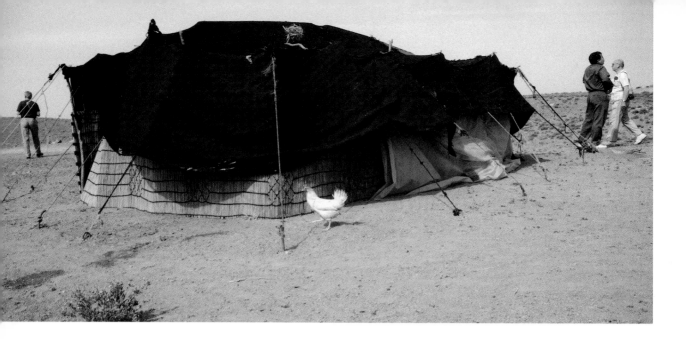

A goat-hair tent used by Qashqai nomads.

Nomads live either in black goat-hair tents or in huts made from willow branches.

The homes of rich Iranians may look elaborate or fussy to American eyes. They are full of overstuffed furniture and crystal chandeliers, and there are lace doilies on the backs of the chairs. Middle-class homes follow the same style but have less furniture. Non-Westernized homes do not have chairs. People sit cross-legged on carpets and eat either at low tables or picnic-style on the floor.

A scene in a non-Westernized home.

Marriage Customs

Iranian men usually marry when they are in their twenties. Most Iranian women marry after they reach the age of sixteen. Villagers tend to marry earlier than educated city dwellers.

Traditionally, most Iranian marriages are arranged. The two families meet for tea, which gives the couple a chance to look each other over and to talk. If they agree to an engagement, the two families get together at a dinner party, where they discuss finances and set a date for the wedding.

Today many Iranians choose their mates from people they have met at university or at work. However, they still ask their families to approve the match.

At the wedding ceremony, a cleric reads from the Qur'an. Then he rubs two pieces of sugar over the bride's veil and asks her three times whether she accepts her husband-to-be. The first two times she says no. The groom's father then agrees to give the new couple some money or property. The third time she is asked, the bride says yes. The couple then sign the marriage contract. Later that day, or perhaps the following day, there is usually a festive dinner at which the bride wears white. The groom wears navy blue or black.

The honeymoon starts several days later. Couples visit various cultural centers or go to a beach or mountain resort. (Women and men swim at separate beaches and ski on different slopes.) Very religious couples also visit the holy city of Mashhad.

Couples partake in a mass wedding ceremony in Tehran.

The Position of Women

Although Iranian women can vote and many of them work outside the home, men hold almost all the important positions in government and business. A woman inherits only half of what a man does. If she appears as a witness in court, her testimony receives only half the weight of a man's. She can be divorced without her knowledge. The age at which a woman can be married has been lowered from fifteen years back to nine.

Iranian women must wear proper Islamic dress when they leave the house. They are segregated, or placed apart, from men in mosques, schools, parks, beaches, polling places, and other public areas. In the cities, they have to ride in the back of a bus. They are not supposed to be alone with any man who is not a family member. They are not even supposed to shake a man's hand unless he is a relative.

On the other hand, Iranian women receive the same education as men, and their job opportunities are increasing. In Iran, unlike some other Muslim nations such as Kuwait and Saudi Arabia, women can drive their own cars and run their own businesses.

Female university students' futures hold increasing job opportunities.

Internet Cafés

"We want to know people in foreign countries, just to communicate and to find out how they live."

"For us, the Internet is a small light inside a very dark tunnel. It allows us to have some contact with the rest of the world."

"Young people in this country are not happy. We are in prison, really. Girls can't ride bicycles in the streets. We can't go out in public with our boyfriends. If you go to a party at someone's house, you are always afraid that the Komiteh guys [public morality police] are going to knock on the door."

These speakers were women in their twenties. They were talking to an American reporter in one of Tehran's Internet cafés in 2001. Since discos and bars are forbidden in Iran, an Internet café is the only place where young city dwellers can socialize.

Tehran at that time had about 1,500 Internet cafés. Just eighteen months earlier, in 2000, the city had only two such cafés. This tremendous growth indicates one of the difficulties that conservative clerics face. They may speak frequently about "cultural invasion and bad ideas from the West," but young people are not paying much attention.

Going to School

Until the 1940s, education in Iran was limited. Only boys attended school. The only subject taught was the Qur'an, which pupils memorized one verse at a time. Only about one out of ten Iranians knew how to read and write.

In 1943, Reza Khan Pahlavi started a Western-style educational system. Schooling was made compulsory for children between the ages of seven and thirteen. Girls as well as boys were expected to attend. Emphasis was placed on teaching pupils how to read and write Farsi. Many children were unable to go to school, either because they lived too far away or because their families needed them to work in the fields. Nevertheless, Iran's literacy rate climbed to about 30 percent.

During the 1960s, Mohammad Reza Shah Pahlavi continued his father's approach. He founded numerous high schools, colleges, universities, and teacher-training schools. He also organized the Literacy Corps. Instead of going into the army, young men who knew how to read and write became teachers in villages that were without schools. By the 1970s, it was estimated that at least half the Iranian population was literate. The figure stood at about 80 percent in early 2002.

Ayatollah Khomeini made several changes in the educational system. He fired about 40,000 teachers, saying that they were not religious enough. Boys and girls are now taught in separate classrooms in elementary school and high school. In addition to religion, the curriculum emphasizes Arabic, the language of the Qur'an. All Iranians must study Arabic for seven years. English is supposed to be taught starting in seventh grade, but there is a shortage of English-speaking teachers.

The school year opens in September and continues through June. The only holiday is a two-week break in March for the New Year. Education is free, but students have to pass a major exam in order to enter high school and another in order to be graduated.

Girls are taught separately at school in Tehran.

Getting into college is difficult. Only about 85,000 students are admitted to Iran's seventy-four public universities each year. There are 1.5 million high school seniors eager to get in. As a result, they spend the year after high school taking special cram courses to prepare for the two-day university entrance exam.

Iran's high unemployment rate is one reason so many Iranians want to go to college. "A degree is the only chance they have for a decent job," one exam coach said. The best students usually major in science and engineering.

Attending college also affects people's place in society. As one young woman explained, "It's completely different for a girl who is in university and a girl who just has a high school diploma. It's different the way employers look at you; it's different the way people at a party look at you."

A few thousand Iranians, from the wealthiest families, either attend one of the country's private universities or study abroad. Surprisingly, about 2,000 Iranians attend colleges in the United States. However, this is a sharp drop from the 51,000 Iranians who were studying in the United States in 1979, just before the Islamic Revolution.

Playing at Sports

Iranians love watching sports events. The most popular spectator sports are soccer and wrestling.

Professional soccer teams are sponsored by private companies. The season lasts from October to June, and games are usually played on Thursdays and Fridays. As many as 100,000

Iran at the Olympics

The 2000 summer Olympic Games, which were held in Sydney, Australia, saw Iran capture three gold medals and one bronze medal. The gold medal winners were Alireza Dabir (pictured above) in freestyle wrestling, and Hossein Tavakkoli and Hossein Rezazadeh (pictured right) in weightlifting. Hadi Saie received a bronze medal in tae kwon do, a martial art.

Rezazadeh's victory was especially impressive. It broke Russia's forty-year winning streak in the super-heavyweight division. Rezazadeh lifted the equivalent of three refrigerators! "I thank God and the Iranian people for my victory," the twenty-two-year-old athlete said.

people jam into a stadium to see a match. In the past only men could attend, but since 2000 women have been allowed to watch, too. In 1998 an Iranian soccer team competed for the World Cup and defeated the U.S. team.

The Iranian national soccer team celebrates winning the King Hussein Cup in 2000.

A young chess player contemplates his next move.

Wrestling Iranian-style is a combination of wrestling and gymnastics. It takes place in an eight-sided building called a *zur khaneh*, or "house of strength." Spectators sit in a ring that is raised above the arena. The wrestlers, wearing only knee-length trousers, enter the arena to the beat of a drum. They swing heavy clubs and chains above their heads to show how strong they are. Then they smear themselves with grease and try to pin their opponent to the ground.

Other popular spectator sports include camel racing and horse racing. Betting on races, however, is now illegal because of the Islamic prohibition of gambling.

A quiet sport is chess. Playing cards, which used to be popular before the Islamic Revolution, is no longer allowed.

Happy New Year

The most important and happiest Iranian festival is *Noruz*, which celebrates the New Year. It starts on March 21, the first day of spring, and lasts for thirteen days.

Preparations for Noruz begin several weeks before the actual day. Around March 6, people plant seeds of wheat or lentils in a shallow dish as a symbol of renewal. Houses are cleaned from top to bottom. Carpets are taken outside to have the dust beaten out of them. People buy new clothes. Business people give their employees presents.

Around March 14, Iranians place a burning candle in each room of their home. The candles create a festive atmosphere. They also symbolize the sacred fire of Zoroastrianism. Many people jump over a small bonfire in the street. This is supposed to cleanse their souls and burn away last year's bad luck.

Also around March 14, Iranians set up a special New Year's table in their home. In the center, they put seven symbolic

Other National Holidays

- February 11 is the anniversary of Khomeini's coming to power in 1979. It is known as the Magnificent Victory of the Islamic Revolution of Iran.

- March 20 is Oil Nationalization Day.

- April 1 is to Iran what the Fourth of July is to the United States. It marks the official establishment of the Islamic Republic of Iran in 1979.

- June 4 is the anniversary of Khomeini's death. It is called the Heart-Rending Departure of the Great Leader of the Islamic Republic of Iran.

- June 5 marks the day in 1963 when Khomeini was arrested after giving a speech in which he urged the world's Muslims to rise up against the superpowers.

- September 8 is the Day of the Martyrs of the Revolution.

foods all starting with the Farsi equivalent of the letter S. The
table also contains either the Qur'an or the poems of Hafiz, as
well as bread, a goldfish, a mirror, and a hard-boiled egg. A leaf
floats in a bowl of water. Tradition says that the moment the
new year arrives, the goldfish will stop swimming, the leaf will
tremble, and the egg will roll across the mirror.

Iranians spend the first twelve days of the new year visit-
ing relatives and friends. They often bring gifts, especially to
children. Everybody eats and drinks. During this period, government offices, schools, and most businesses are closed.

The thirteenth day of the new year is considered unlucky.
To get rid of the bad luck, Iranians throw out the dish of green
shoots. Then they go on a family picnic outdoors.

**A family gathers to celebrate
the Iranian New Year.**

Timeline

<table>
<tr><th>Iranian History</th><th></th><th>World History</th><th></th></tr>
<tr><td>Iranian villagers practice farming, herding, pottery making, and metalworking.</td><td>6000 B.C.E.</td><td></td><td></td></tr>
<tr><td>Elamite culture is established.</td><td>3000 B.C.E.</td><td></td><td></td></tr>
<tr><td></td><td></td><td>2500 B.C.</td><td>Egyptians build the Pyramids and the Sphinx in Giza.</td></tr>
<tr><td>Indo-Europeans enter Iran.</td><td>1500 B.C.E.</td><td></td><td></td></tr>
<tr><td>First Persian Empire is established under Achaemenid dynasty.</td><td>500 B.C.E.</td><td>563 B.C.</td><td>The Buddha is born in India.</td></tr>
<tr><td>Alexander the Great conquers Persian Empire.</td><td>336–333 B.C.E.</td><td></td><td></td></tr>
<tr><td>Seleucids rule Iran.</td><td>323–250 B.C.E.</td><td></td><td></td></tr>
<tr><td>Parthians rule Iran.</td><td>250–224 B.C.E.</td><td></td><td></td></tr>
<tr><td>Second Persian Empire, under Sassanian dynasty.</td><td>224–627</td><td></td><td></td></tr>
<tr><td></td><td></td><td>A.D. 313</td><td>The Roman emperor Constantine recognizes Christianity.</td></tr>
<tr><td></td><td></td><td>610</td><td>The prophet Muhammad begins preaching a new religion called Islam.</td></tr>
<tr><td>Arabs rule Iran.</td><td>652–908</td><td>1054</td><td>The Eastern (Orthodox) and Western (Roman) Churches break apart.</td></tr>
<tr><td>Turks rule Iran.</td><td>1040–1220</td><td>1066</td><td>William the Conqueror defeats the English in the Battle of Hastings.</td></tr>
<tr><td></td><td></td><td>1095</td><td>Pope Urban II proclaims the First Crusade.</td></tr>
<tr><td></td><td></td><td>1215</td><td>King John seals the Magna Carta.</td></tr>
<tr><td></td><td></td><td>1300s</td><td>The Renaissance begins in Italy.</td></tr>
<tr><td>Mongols invade Iran.</td><td>1220–1380</td><td>1347</td><td>The Black Death sweeps through Europe.</td></tr>
<tr><td></td><td></td><td>1453</td><td>Ottoman Turks capture Constantinople, conquering the Byzantine Empire.</td></tr>
<tr><td></td><td></td><td>1492</td><td>Columbus arrives in North America.</td></tr>
</table>

Iranian History		World History	
Safavid dynasty rules Iran.	1501–1722	1500s	The Reformation leads to the birth of Protestantism.
Nadir Shah seizes Persian throne.	1736	1776	The Declaration of Independence is signed.
		1789	The French Revolution begins.
Qajar dynasty rules Iran.	1794–1925	1865	The American Civil War ends.
Oil is discovered.	1908	1914	World War I breaks out.
		1917	The Bolshevik Revolution brings communism to Russia.
Reza Khan seizes throne and establishes Pahlavi dynasty.	1925	1929	Worldwide economic depression begins.
		1939	World War II begins, following the German invasion of Poland.
Reza Khan abdicates in favor of son Mohammad Reza.	1941	1945	World War II ends.
Oil industry is nationalized.	1951	1957	The Vietnam War starts.
		1969	Humans land on the moon.
		1975	The Vietnam War ends.
Islamic Republic of Iran is proclaimed; Iranian militants seize U.S. embassy.	1979	1979	Soviet Union invades Afghanistan.
Iran-Iraq War.	1980–1988	1983	Drought and famine in Africa.
Ayatollah Ruhollah Khomeini dies.	1989	1989	The Berlin Wall is torn down, as communism crumbles in Eastern Europe.
		1991	Soviet Union breaks into separate states.
		1992	Bill Clinton is elected U.S. president.
Seyed Mohammad Khatami is elected president.	1997		
Seyed Mohammad Khatami is reelected president.	2001	2000	George W. Bush is elected U.S. president.

Fast Facts

Official name:	Islamic Republic of Iran (Jomhuri-e Eslami-e Iran)
Capital:	Tehran
Official language:	Farsi (or Persian)

Tehran

Iran's flag

Zagros Mountains

Official religion:	Shi'ite Islam
Year of founding:	1979
National anthem:	*"Soroude jomhuri-e Eslimi-e Iran"* ("Anthem of the Islamic Republic of Iran")
Government:	Islamic republic
Chief of state:	Velayat-e faqih (Islamic jurist)
Head of state:	President
Area and dimensions of country:	Almost 636,000 square miles (1,648,000 sq km)
Greatest distance north to south:	810 miles (1,296 km)
Greatest distance east to west:	860 miles (1,376 km)
Land borders:	Armenia, Azerbaijan, and Turkmenistan to the north; Afghanistan and Pakistan to the east; Iraq and Turkey to the west
Water borders:	Caspian Sea to the north; Persian Gulf and Gulf of Oman to the south
Highest elevation:	Mount Demavand, 18,934 feet (5,771 m)
Lowest elevation:	92 feet (28 m) below sea level, along the coast of the Caspian Sea
Highest average temperature:	122°F (50°C)
Lowest average temperature:	-20°F (-29°C)

Great stairway of Persepolis

Currency

Highest average annual precipitation: 40–60 inches (100–150 cm), in the coastal lowland along the Caspian Sea

Lowest average annual precipitation: 5 inches (12.7 cm), in the deserts

National population: 66–75 million

Population of largest cities (1996 census):

Tehran (2002 est.)	10,000,000
Mashhad	1,887,405
Esfahan	1,266,072
Tabriz	1,191,043
Shiraz	1,053,025

Famous landmarks:
- ▶ *Azadi Tower*, Tehran
- ▶ *Blue Mosque*, Tabriz
- ▶ *Citadel and walled city*, Bam
- ▶ *Cliff carvings*, Bisotun (or Behistun)
- ▶ *Khaju Bridge*, Esfahan
- ▶ *Persepolis*
- ▶ *Tomb of Imam Reza*, Mashhad

Industry: Iran's most important industrial product by far is oil, followed by textiles. The country contains some manufacturing plants that produce automobiles, cement, fertilizer, steel, and sugar. Tourism, which used to be a major industry, has declined since the Islamic Revolution.

Currency: The rial. Each rial equals 100 dinars. Ten rials form one toman. As of January 20, 2002, 1,755 rials were equal to U.S.$1.

Garden at the tomb of
poet Saadi

Cyrus the Great

**Common words
and phrases:**

Salam	Hello
Khoda hafez	Goodbye
Hale shoma chetor-e?	How are you?
Lotfan.	Please.
Mersi.	Thank you.
Khakesh me konan.	You're welcome.
bale	yes
na	no
nan	bread
gusht	meat
mast	yogurt
sabzi	vegetables
miveh	fruit

Famous Iranians:

Cyrus the Great (600–529 B.C.E.)
*Achaemenid ruler who
conquered Babylon*

Darius I (558–486 B.C.E.)
*Achaemenid ruler who built
a large road system*

Ferdosi (about 940–1020)
Poet who wrote Iran's national epic

Shah Abbas the Great (1557–1629)
Safavid ruler who built Esfahan

Omar Khayyám (1047?–1123?)
Poet, best known for Rubaiyat

Ayatollah Ruhollah Khomeini (1900–1989)
Leader of the Islamic Revolution

To Find Out More

Nonfiction

▶ Gordon, Matthew S. *Islam*. New York: Facts on File, 1991.

▶ Husain, A. *Revolution in Iran*. Vero Beach, FL: Rourke Enterprises, 1988.

▶ Lyle, Garry. *Iran*. Philadelphia: Chelsea House Publishers, 1999.

▶ McMillan, Dianne M. *Ramadan and Id al-Fitr*. Hillside, NJ: Enslow, 1994.

▶ Moritz, Patricia M. and Philip Bader. *Iran*. Vero Beach, FL: Rourke Publishing, 2002.

▶ Rajendra, Vijeya and Gisela Kaplan. *Iran*. New York: Marshall Cavendish, 1993.

▶ Spencer, William. *Iran: Land of the Peacock Throne*. New York: Marshall Cavendish, 1997.

Web Sites

▶ **Iran**
www.cia.gov/cia/publications/
factbook/geos/ir.html
*Facts about Iran including its
geography, people, and government.*

▶ **Persian Heritage**
www.persiansite.com
*Covers the history of Iran both before
and after the coming of Islam.*

▶ **History of Iran**
www.mage.com
*A timeline of Iranian history with
numerous illustrations.*

Iranian Trade Association
▶ www. farsinet.com
*Covers Iranian art and collectibles,
history, and literature.*

Index

Page numbers in *italics* indicate illustrations.

Meet the Author

MIRIAM GREENBLATT writes books about history. Several chapters in some of her books have been about the first Persian Empire, which flourished more than 2,000 years ago. Other chapters have dealt with the magnificent buildings put up by Shah Abbas the Great. "As a result," she says, "I always wanted to see Persepolis and Esfahan. I was certain they would be glamorous places to visit, and they turned out

that way. Persepolis in particular. Although only ruins remain, you can still imagine what the city was like in its glory." Her trip to Iran in 1999 covered some 3,000 miles. "Thank goodness we had an air-conditioned bus," she says, "especially since the women travelers all had to wear proper Islamic dress. It was quite an experience."

Photo Credits